A BUSINESS JOURNALIST'S SHORT GUIDE TO WRITING AT WORK

Quickly Create Great Messages

A business journalist with 40+ years of experience reveals writing techniques to help you in the workplace.

Peter J. Brennan

Howtowriteatwork@gmail.com

A short guide on how to write at work

Copyright 2022

ISBN: 9780990792512

1st Edition

For classes, private lessons: Howtowriteatwork@gmail.com

DEDICATION

This book is dedicated to every student who fell asleep during their grammar classes and their frustrated teachers.

ACKNOWLEDGMENTS

The author wishes to acknowledge the many editors who strove to improve ~~my~~ his articles.

Introduction

1 minute read.

This introduction is short, for those who want to immediately start learning. Part 2 introduction will provide inspiration on why you should complete this course.

This book is version two, which includes exam questions at the end of each chapter to help you remember the key points. It also corrects some of my own errors made when writing the first edition! Even professionals make writing mistakes.

This book will help you improve your writing in less than three hours. Guaranteed or your money back. It's divided into 11 short chapters that each will take less than 15 minutes to read. You can read each chapter on your cell phone, tablet or monitor.

At the end of each chapter is a short quiz. My suggestion is to write down each answer on a pad of paper. Studies have shown that the physical process of writing helps the reader remember much better.

The book also has professional tips spread throughout the book; they are also repeated in Chapter 11. Chapter 10 includes a 65-point checklist for your writing. If you master each professional tip, the 25 essential parts of grammar in Chapter 1 and the 65-point checklist, you are on your way to writing well.

You can reach me on LinkedIn where I blog -- feel free to leave comments! I

For classes, private lessons: Howtowriteatwork@gmail.com

occasionally teach webinars and at corporate offices.

After 11 lessons, spread out over two weeks, your writing will improve. It certainly won't get worse. I guarantee it. Or your money back.

ˈ

The Why

2-minute read

I've been a journalist now for more than 40 years.

You might be surprised to learn that I'm not the greatest at grammar. I still make mistakes. I often reread my stories after publication and think, I could have written more clearly this sentence or that paragraph.

So why should you read this book?

I've learned a lot of writing techniques over those 40 years.

Altogether, I estimate that I've written more than 30,000 articles that have appeared in periodicals like The New York Times, the Economist and the Washington Post. I've spoken on radio and appeared on television on networks including CNN, BBC, CBC and Bloomberg News.

In my career, I've covered everything from the 2008 financial crisis to earthquakes and wars in Central America.

I spent a decade covering Latin America while residing in Venezuela and Costa Rica.

The Ohio State University awarded me a Kiplinger Fellowship, which gave him a full-ride scholarship to earn a master's in journalism. I wrote a thesis on the economic impact of illegal immigrants in the U.S., a paper that famed economist Art Laffer published.

I spent 15 years at Bloomberg News, interviewing tech icons like Steve Jobs, Michael Dell and Ted Waitt. I was often the first to send headlines to Wall Street, causing stocks to move by hundreds of millions of dollars.

After covering the best and brightest on Wall Street, I wrote a book on personal finance for regular consumers, "A simple guide to wealth: 7 steps to become rich(er)." Both books are available on Amazon.com.

I've taught writing courses, such as *How to Turn Numbers into the Narrative* at the prestigious Chapman University's School of Business in Southern California.

As of this writing, I'm the Executive Editor at the Orange County Business Journal where I assign and edit many of the articles about this Southern California province that has an economy the size of Finland's. Note how the previous sentence created an image to describe the economy I cover. I write articles about banks, insurance companies, stockbrokers, wealth managers and anyone involved in the business of money.

I hope you enjoy this course. Suggestions are always welcomed. If you're not satisfied, I'll give you your money back. No questions asked (but an explanation appreciated!)

Part 2

Were you asleep during grammar class in school? Maybe daydreaming? Thought you'd never need to use the skill of writing.

This book emphasizes how to write at work. It includes tips on how to make you look smarter.

The biggest problem with most grammar books is they are geared to young students who dream of the Great American Novel. These students want to learn the secrets of how to write well. They explore prose and poetry that sings. They marvel at the literary devices of Moby Dick. They study how to build magical metaphors to send hidden messages that once cracked, thrill readers and English professors. They are excited to learn the significance of the Mississippi in Huckleberry Finn.

People who write for business pursue different goals. They want to communicate with their bosses or their employees or their customers. They aim to convey clear and concise messages for something as simple as emails or meaty as a five-page proposal to convince people of their viewpoints. They need to know what works. I witnessed an investment committee decide to invest $500 million because of a 750-word paper ghost written by a colleague at Pimco for two portfolio managers.

In writing for business, ambiguity is the enemy. Metaphors, soliloquies and grammatical errors are to be found and shot.

People who are thrust into business may suddenly realize there are mistakes in their emails to bosses or employees.

Ever wonder why knowing the difference between the use of good and well is the sign of an educated person? Ever confuse their with there? How about it's with its? Don't understand the verb-subject agreement? And maybe you never heard of parallelism? Ever hear someone snicker if you say "irregardless"?

These errors may cause others to wonder if we are as smart as we all pretend to be. Someone may be snotty behind our backs, saying we are splitting the infinitive! We might wonder if we got passed over for promotions because of grammatical mistakes in our messages. Ever grimace about the boss who sends a message full of grammatical mistakes? The surest way to look dumb is to write poorly.

If you think you write good, this book is for you. If you didn't understand the irony in the previous sentence, this book really is for you!

This book is for people in business or the government who don't love grammar but realize their path to success is to write well enough and avoid those silly errors that it seems like everyone else knows.

How many were daydreaming in 10th grade when our old fuddy-duddy English teachers taught the verb-subject agreement? I know I was. In college, all of us picked up bad habits such as the student parlor trick of stretching a 500-word essay into 2,000 words.

What are we to do?

You can brush up on your grammar but trying to pick the right book on Amazon is daunting. And too many of the books aren't targeted toward business. Many of you don't have the time to slog through a thick book on grammar and would be bored stiff if you do.

Who has the time for a 10-week refresher course taught by someone who would rather be writing the great American novel? You can hire your own personal editor (I am available!).

Presto – "The Quick Business Writing Guide" is a short primer to help you.

This book will teach readers how to sharpen their English skills in 11 chapters that range from the most important grammatical terms in Chapter 1 to verb tenses to parallelism in Chapter 4 to headlines in Chapter 9. The final chapter is a list of hard-won techniques used by professional editors and writers.

This book doesn't cover every single grammatical issue. There are other books up to 600 pages thick that explain in excruciating detail the guidelines for prepositional phrases or subjunctive clauses. I read many grammatical books of such length for both my professional career and to make sure I didn't miss something significant in this book.

This book will teach executives the subtle techniques employed by journalists to improve their writing. It's a quick read with practice questions and something to have on your desk for reference. Why me above all your other choices?

After 40-plus years in journalism, I've published more than 30,000 articles. The world's most prestigious publications like The New York Times, the Washington Post and Die Welt have published my articles. On Wall Street, I've written headlines and articles that have moved the market capitalization of publicly traded companies by hundreds of millions of dollars.

I've learned techniques that you can also employ to improve your writing skills. These skills won't win you a Pulitzer Prize, but they will permit a bigger award: the ability to communicate.

I want to share an embarrassing secret as well. The editors during my career would be shocked to read that I am writing a book that includes grammar. I'm not the best at this subject. I was the journalist who got the scoops and told great stories. I left the technical boring grammar stuff to editors to straighten out. Grammar was too hard, had too many exceptions and didn't make much sense. Besides, that is what editors are for – to fix any errors in my copy. I grew up in Hawaii speakin' da kine pidgin, a broken-down English where anything went.

That attitude was a big mistake in my career, one that I believe cost me jobs and pay raises. It took years of editors scolding me about common errors that you will learn in this book.

9

For classes, private lessons: Howtowriteatwork@gmail.com

This book is written from the viewpoint of someone who is not the very best in the field of grammar, but who has learned to appreciate its many nuances and flexibility and to love the editors who improve my writing. After years of publishing articles, I can pinpoint the top mistakes when writing.

I've learned from the best, including Matthew Winkler, founder of Bloomberg News, and Emma Moody, one of my former bosses and as of this writing one of the most important editors at The Wall Street Journal. My journalism professor Lynn Ludlow worked at the San Francisco Examiner where he taught reporting to the grandchildren of William Randolph Hearst. My editor at the Orange County Business Journal, Rick Reiff, is a Pulitzer Prize winner who helped edit this course.

I believe this course will teach you. If not, I'll refund your money. Guaranteed.

1.

Five important things to remember before writing

5-minute read

Before writing, ask yourself the following five main questions:

1.) What is the main point of this email, blog or article? Can I sum it up in one or two sentences?
2.) What tense will I use? Past or present or future? Using the past tense will save a lot of headaches in the long run.
3.) Who will read this writing? Will it be government workers, so I should be more formal? Will it be employees under me? Or my bosses? Will the public read this?
4.) Will the people I respect be embarrassed if they read it? If so, don't write it.
5.) What has been written before on this subject?

For instance, if the message is to your boss, it can be more sophisticated than if it is for the employees who work for you. Generally, a boss will have worked in your area for years so knows well many aspects of your business. If your subordinates have less experience than you or your bosses, tailor the message to them.

If you are writing to your employees, be a cheerleader. One technique used is that instead of directly criticizing the actions of your employees, compliment them on something they did well and then make a point about what you want the employees to do better.

For example, one of our managers sent out a companywide message like this:

> ***You guys are slobs in the kitchen! Please clean up your messes!!!***

The manager who wrote the message was inexperienced in communication. That person accused the entire staff of being slobs. Obviously, it was only a few people who were the slobs. How to phrase the message?

> ***Hello team! Our kitchen is often looking great so thank you.***
> ***However, there were a couple times in the past week when food was left over in the sink – yuck! This note is a quick reminder to clean up the kitchen after using it.***
> ***It'd really be uplifting to know that everyone loves a clean kitchen.***

If you are writing to your bosses or your employees, convince them of your viewpoint. A common technique is explaining the problem, the possible solutions and which solution you think is best and why.

The four best words to elicit communications are: What do you think?

If you're writing to your Mom or someone close, you don't want to sound stiff and formal as though you're writing a letter to the taxman. You can end the message with the salutation *love*.

However, in the workplace, no one wants to end a message to bosses with *love*.
For years, I didn't have any salutation at the end of an email. Instead, I left it blank. Tough guy journalist was I. When I had a six-month content writing gig at the bond giant Pimco, my boss told me the polite salutation to use was ***Best***. I was surprised; I learned - - adapt to your workplace.

Such messages are the low-hanging fruit. The tougher message is to the public outside your company, such as through a blog or an article. Always ask yourself: Who is your target audience

When I edit financial blogs, I know readers want to know details of how other people are investing such as the specific names of stocks or bonds or industries. They are looking for signs from other people of the investment climate, whether the writer is bullish or bearish. Generalized comments, such as "We expect the economy to get better," are a dime a dozen. When does the subject expect the economy to improve – next month, next quarter, in three years? Be specific in what future actions you see coming. In short, readers want to know how to make more money themselves.

Say your specialty is cosmetics for women. Your readers want to know how to look more beautiful and hide blemishes. They are seeking details about the products you are reviewing such as the names, prices, availability, weather it works best in, etc.

Don't try mixing the two. A writer who has become known for financial blogs shouldn't veer off to which cosmetic looks best. The cosmetics blog writer discussing muni bonds loses readers.

Know your audience.

PRO TIP 1 – Write about subjects that you know. Don't opine on popular issues in the media that you may not be fully versed in.

History

Know your history or you are condemned to repeat it, to paraphrase the familiar saying.

The same goes for writing.

Know what has been written before you write it. For example, if you are writing an email to your employees, study the previous five emails to your employees. You don't want to tell them something they have already read. You want something new – which is why it's called news.

I've seen so many emails that are templates of prior emails. I don't bother to read them. Why? Because I don't think the sender has something new to say. Don't make every email start the same way. Be sure to say something new in the subject line.

When I write an article, I read what the other media is saying about the subject. That way, I'm not just repeating them, but I can quickly recognize what is different and hence what is new.

Word Count

How long is your message?

If you're writing a sentence or two, it's not a problem for an email. It's not enough for an article though. How many words should be in a sentence or an email or a blog?

It's important to tell the readers how long they should expect to be reading. A reader of a book understands that it might be days. A reader of a blog wants to finish the article in 1 minute or so. The reader of a newspaper article may expect two to four minutes.

At the beginning of each chapter in this book is an estimated time to read. That sets the tone for how long a person can be in the chapter.

Let's start with the basics.

Sentence:

A concise sentence usually contains about eight to 12 words. Sentences from 12 to 25 words increase the potential of becoming muddled. Any sentence longer than 25 words verges on the territory of James Joyce's "Ulysses." Avoid sentences longer than 25 words or risk losing the reader.

Sentence length isn't a hard and fast rule. If you like to write short concise sentences, critics will say you are writing for simpletons. Thank goodness we have Hemmingway to prove the beauty of short sentences.

Long sentences are often the domain of professional writers who make a living at it. Long sentences cause the reader to stop and ponder the meaning of what the writer Is trying to say. For business writing, ambiguity is a killer of messages. People will give up reading what you are trying to say.

PRO TIP 2: If you want to mix it up, use short sentences with a few long sentences thrown in. Don't use long sentences with a few short ones.

Paragraph:

University professors love 'em long. So do some authors.

For business, let's copy a technique long employed by newspapers and magazines: Keep each paragraph to one sentence or maybe two. Three might be the exception. Do not use four sentences or more in a paragraph.

The reason is that newspaper stories often had a narrow width. Anything longer than two sentences made the paragraph look longer than it is. Newspapers and magazines successfully deployed this method, which still has a lot of validity.

Nowadays, with people reading on their cell phones, this technique will help avoid the appearance of a paragraph that takes up the entire screen.

Email

Up to 200 words, which is about six to eight paragraphs. A longer email is harder to follow, particularly on cell phones and when a group of people starts responding.

Blog

200 to 500 words. Blogs are meant to be short and to one point. I've seen many blogs go over 1,000 words. Don't put such lengthy articles into a blog section. Publish them elsewhere on your web page like in the thought leadership section.

Sponsored content:

About 400 to 800 words. These are articles you can pay to place on the websites of popular publications like Barron's. Treat it like an article that you would want to read. It's a surprisingly effective way to get your message out.

Newspaper article

Most are 500 words to 1,000 words. When I worked at Bloomberg, we had a guideline limiting articles to 850 words. Sometimes, great stories ran over 1,000 words. It was difficult to reduce the word count, but the guideline often made articles better by eliminating the least interesting or newsworthy items.

Magazine/trade articles

An in-depth article for a magazine can be 1,000 to 4,000 words.

White paper

About 3,000 to 7,000 words. Any author should realize such papers are synonyms for wonky and boring to those outside the profession.

White papers won't get as much readership as say a blog. White papers are written for colleagues in similar fields. At Pimco, the upper management wondered why their top analysts wrote white papers that could give away trade secrets to competitors. The answer was that these wonky researchers wanted to let other researchers know about their serious research, albeit at a corporation instead of a university.

Book

About 200 to 300 words per page. So, a 200-page book may have 40,000 to 60,000 words.

Writing a book sounds intimidating because it is. But when the book is broken down into chapters, it is more manageable. A chapter can be 2,000 to 5,000 words, like the length of a magazine article.

Don't ever think you need to write a book to be considered a good writer. Good writing is about quality – not quantity.

PRO TIP 3: One high-level executive at Pimco

was inspired to write an article of 1,000 to 2,000 words and then expected his company to publish it on the company website. The problem was this executive didn't realize his article would anger a major client. Executives could save themselves time by sending only a 100-to-200-word pitch to the managers of the websites. The website manager, sometimes known as the communications director or content editor, can guide the executive to the appropriate subject matter and word length.

Remember that communications executives are trying to build an image of the company. Employees, including executives, who go rogue are a detriment to the company. A pitch provides the author and the content editor the opportunity to develop this image.

Before you publish something that may embarrass your company, ask yourself, "Is my opinion on this subject worth my annual salary?

PRO TIP 4: If you write a book, you will be introduced at public forums as the person who wrote the book on subject X. However, don't consider a book a future big revenue stream. There are only about 800 authors in the U.S. who can make a full-time living writing books. Instead, think of a book on your field of expertise as a good way to market yourself. And be pleasantly surprised if people read your book.

Quiz:

Research has shown that the actual act of writing down an answer in longhand will help you remember the main points more than mere guessing at a multiple-choice answer.

As a result, look at these questions and write down your answers in longhand. The answers are in this chapter.

1.) How many words should a concise sentence be?
2.) What is the problem if your email always has the same subject line?
3.) What are the five things to consider before writing?
4.) What are the four best words to elicit communication?
5.) What should you not write about?
6.) How long are most newspaper articles?
7.) How many words should an email not exceed?
8.) How many sentences per paragraph?
9.) Why is it important to limit the number of sentences per paragraph?
10.) Why should you work with your company's communications manager before publishing something?
11.) Who will read your emails? Blogs? Articles? White papers?

2.

Verb Tenses

2 minute read

Verb tenses are as confusing as parrots in jungles. One moment, you think you've spotted the correct tense and the next moment, you lose sight of them. Then the tenses squawk and you're left wondering what the hell to do.

Erroneous shifts in tenses are key mistakes that may cause readers to misunderstand the writing.

We in the media haven't made it any easier.

For example, headlines almost always use present tense to give their articles a sense of urgency. However, the stories themselves are often in the past tense. You can see this in every major newspaper.

Magazines often use present tenses in their articles to hide the fact that the news they are writing about is often weeks if not months or years old.

For our purposes – try to keep all tenses in the past. This will save you a lot of grief. The exception of course is when you discuss the future.

Pro Tip 5: Hundreds of different irregular verbs have odd tenses that can befuddle you as easily as a tax bill. Rather than be intimidated by dozens of examples, stay in the past tense.

Ask yourself, what is wrong with this sentence:

A short guide on how to write at work

Jenna moved to Nevada where she works at our rival company's factory after she was working at our factory in California and now she will return to work for us in Utah.

The sentence has four different verb tenses. Try to avoid shifting them in the same sentence. This will lead to confusion.

Don't lose the tense. In the following sentence, the writer confuses the reader as to whether Jenna is still working at the factory:

Jenna moves to Nevada where she worked at our rival company's factory after she was working at our factory in California and she will have returned to work for us in Utah.

Keeping tenses similar in the same sentence will help you avoid confusion. If you need to use different tenses, consider a second sentence.

Jenna worked at our factory in California and then moved to a rival's factory in Nevada. She will return to work for us at our factory in Utah.

An easy way to remember is to go in chronological order. In other words, start at oldest and end at the newest.

Pro Tip 6: Be aware of tenses that shift within your sentences or your story.

No need to double up on past tense. Take the sentence for example:

Last month saw the dollar strengthened.

Since the first verb is past tense, you don't have to make the second verb past as well. Instead, use:

Last month saw the dollar strengthen.

Chapter 2 Quiz:

Write the answers in longhand:

1.) Are most headlines present or past tenses?
2.) Why are magazine articles often in the present tense?
3.) What's the best guideline for tenses?
4.) What is wrong with this sentence?

John works at the Widget Corp. two years ago and now Gadget LLC employed him.

5.) Correct this sentence:

John saw the person strengthened the fort.

3.

The Verb-Subject Agreement

10-minute read

A sentence can be complicated, complex and overwhelming. We can add tons of color like adjectives and phrases and clauses and adverbs and conjunctions and run the sentence on forever, like the sentence you are about to finish reading if I ever decide to put a period at the end. There!

We don't want to write novels or movie scripts. We're writing for business. We want clarity.

Have you ever read the instructions for a product and wondered, how the hell does this product work?

Here are nine ideas for verbs, subjects, agreements and all that stuff.

1. The Three Basic Parts of a Sentence:

> The most important part of writing is to understand the three basic parts of a sentence.
>
> A.) Subject: a word or group of words doing the action of the verb. The subject can be a person or thing and is the main reason for the sentence. In this example, John is the subject:

John delivered the book.

B.) Verb: The action word in this sentence is delivered.

John *delivered* the book.

C.) Direct object: It directly follows a verb and receives the action conveyed by the verb. For example, the object in this sentence is the book.

John delivered *the book.*

These three parts are the basic building blocks of a sentence. Everything else is superfluous. If we cannot identify the subject, verb and direct object, we are lost when writing a sentence. Learn to spot these three items and try to eliminate all else.

Pro Tip 7: A short comment about a sentence fragment. The previous sentence is a fragment. It looks like a sentence, but it doesn't have a verb. It is the opposite of a run-on sentence. A fragment is best used if you want to emphasize a point.

2. One Main Idea Per Sentence

Study this sentence to determine the subject, verb and direct object.

Before the rain began, John, who is an avaricious reader and enjoyed spending hours in the library, quickly delivered the elegant, thick books, which were about 300 pages each, to the library on the far side of the university near Main Street.

A short guide on how to write at work

Our goal is one principal idea per sentence. We might stretch for two main ideas, but the reader gets lost if there are three, four or five ideas in a sentence. Think of the subject, the verb and the object as the one main idea of the sentence. Consider the prior example. Let's count how many ideas there are:

1.) Before the rain began,
2.) John delivered the book
3.) who is an avaricious reader
4.) and enjoyed spending hours in the library,
5.) quickly
6.) the elegant, thick
7.) which were about 300 pages each,
8.) to the library
9.) on the far side of the university
10.) near Main Street.

There are 10 ideas in this sentence. It's too much. How do you break the sentence down?

The first question to ask yourself: what information do the readers need?

For example, if your readers are students on the campus, they probably know the library is on the far side of the campus near Main Street.

If the readers are not familiar with the campus, are you expecting the readers to visit and will need directions? If not, cut out the directions. That gets rid of two ideas.

Do the readers need to know John is an avaricious reader who likes to spend hours in the library? Is it important to your message? Do we need thick when we say the books are 300 pages each?

Before the rain began, John quickly delivered the elegant books, which were about 300 pages each, to the university's library.

Let's count the ideas in this sentence:
1.) Before the rain began,
2.) John delivered the books
3.) quickly
4.) which were about 300 pages each
5.) to the university's library.

We're now down to five ideas, which are more manageable. The main idea is clear, and the rest of the sentence modifies it. If we want to keep some of the other elements of the original sentence, we can split it into two sentences.

Before the rain began, John quickly delivered the books to the university's library. John had checked out the elegant books, which were about 300 pages each, from the library located near Main Street.

3. The Verb-Subject Agreement

Which is correct?

A group of players are on the field.
A group of players is on the field.

It's easy to miss since the plural players is next to the verb. The second sentence is correct because group is singular. If you don't pay attention to the verb-subject agreement, there is a lot of tsk-tsk from readers who know this rule. Getting the verb-subject agreement right is a sign of a good education.

Once you know the verb-subject agreement, it's relatively simple to spot. In short, the agreement

A short guide on how to write at work

is to make sure the subject agrees in number with the verb. For example:

John counts the sheep.
John and Mike count the sheep.

In the first example, John is singular, so the verb takes an s at the end. In the second example, John and Mike are plural so the verb doesn't use the s.

It gets complicated when you write a long sentence where the verb is far away from the subject. That's why it's important to identify the subject and main verb of each sentence.

Many rules surround the verb-subject agreement. For example, nor and or take singular verbs. And takes the plural verb. Consider these examples:

Neither Bob nor Mary has the book.
Neither Bob or Mary has the book.
Both Bob and Mary have the book.

If one subject is plural, take the subject closest to the verb to decide if singular or plural.

Neither Robert nor other members of the team are excellent athletes.

Sometimes the verb-subject agreement isn't clear. Say the subject comes after the verb. What to do?

Attached is my cover letter and resume.

Should be:

Attached are my cover letter and resume.

27

The verb-subject agreement has more than 20 exceptions, such as money (singular when specific, plural when vague) or time (singular).

Truth be told – grammar rules can drive anyone up the wall. If in doubt, come back to this section or Google the proper use.

Here are three basic recommendations for the verb-subject agreement:

A.) Does it sound correct?

Ham and eggs is a good breakfast.
Ham and eggs are a good breakfast.

According to grammar rules, the latter is correct. Try reading it aloud. The former sounds better. We can justify this by treating ham and eggs as a singular unit. It's up to the writer and editor to determine which form doesn't make the reader pause.

Consider this:

Ham, eggs and bacon is a great breakfast.
Ham, eggs and bacon are a great breakfast.

The latter sounds better.

B.) Change the subjects to plural.

C.) If in doubt, rewrite it.

4. Confusing the Subject and Direct Object

Don't make the subject of the sentence look like a direct object. Consider this sentence:

Since Larry enjoys driving, the forklift is the ideal job for him.

What is the subject? The forklift? A reader might think it's Larry. But Larry is in the clause, so he cannot be the subject. The subject should depend on what the writer wants to say. This topic is where writing becomes fun, like a golfer deciding which iron to use in a certain situation. In this example, we make clear that the forklift is the subject and Larry is the object.

The forklift is the ideal job for Larry since he enjoys driving.

If you want to emphasize Larry as the subject, simply rewrite:

Larry enjoys driving so the ideal job for him is the forklift.

Or you can make job the subject.

Larry's ideal job is driving the forklift.

Here's a simple technique to make people enjoy your writing: the forklift won't read the above sentence. Someone, maybe Larry, will read it. Make Larry the subject, the most important part of the sentence. People appreciate the attention.

Pro Tip 8: A word about there. If the sentence begins with there, it's a sign of a weak sentence. Look for the subject after the verb. Rewrite to put the subject before the verb. If you must use there, make sure the verb agrees in there is or there are:
Poor: There are two ways people achieve no-closing costs mortgages.

Better: People can achieve no-closing costs mortgages in two ways.

5. Commas are the keys to finding run-on sentences

Remember the old saying: Don't try this at home. The same can be said for long sentences you read in a magazine. That sentence was written by a professional writer. Don't try to copy him or her because you might end up with a run-on sentence that keeps going and going and going like a bunny rabbit that never stops. Run-on sentences should be erased from the computer screen and ostracized.

How do you spot them?

If the sentence has five or more ideas, chances are good that it's a run-on sentence. If the subject is far from the verb or the verb is far from the object, it could be a run-on sentence. Commas are a big clue to help you catch run-on sentences. In this sentence, count how many words separate the subject from the noun.

Paris, a beautiful city full of wondrous lights and a lazy river running through the middle of it, strives to maintain its old buildings.

Seventeen words separate Paris from the verb strives. The comma tells you a phrase you can delete. How many words separate the verb from the object in the following sentence?

Paris, a beautiful city full of wondrous lights and a lazy river running through the middle of it, strives to maintain, in a way that other cities don't and cannot understand, its buildings.

Twelve words separate *strives* from *buildings*. Besides the verb being too far from the object, the reader may misconstrue the writing to think that Paris understands its building rather than the writer trying to say Paris maintains its buildings. Break down the sentence to concentrate on the subject, verb and object.

Paris strives to maintain its buildings.

Then ask yourself: Do we need to say the obvious that Paris is a beautiful city with a lazy river running through it? In business writing, most likely not. Then ask: Do we really need to make a subjective statement that other cities don't maintain their buildings? Maybe so.

Paris strives to maintain its buildings in a way that other cities don't and cannot understand.

In this way, we add that Paris works harder than other cities to maintain its buildings. A journalist would add a statistic to back up this statement like a maintenance budget compared to other cities.

6. This and That Are Bad Subjects

Don't make this or that the subject. For example:

This is a superb book.

This becomes the subject and book becomes the object. The reader can get lost by trying to figure out what this stands for. Instead, try:

This book is superb.

The book becomes the subject, making it easier for the reader to identify what is being discussed.
Remember This and that are pronouns. It's not always clear what they are referring to.

7. Abstract nouns are bad subjects

Try to make a person or thing as the subject. For example:

Sorrow is commonplace in war zones.

Sorrow is abstract. Try this:

People in war zones often feel sorrow.

8. Subjects before Verbs

Try to place the subject before the verb. The exception is asking a question where the subject can be on the right of the verb. Grammar experts call this interrogative.
Inverted sentences are commonplace. Seek them out and rewrite:

Here is an atlas of the world along with a guidebook.
An atlas of the world and a guidebook are here.

9. Plural is Easier to Remember Than Singular

A big problem is sentences that start as singular and switch to plural. Try to write plural for everything. For example:

A boy plays basketball.
Boys play basketball.

10. Indefinite pronouns.

These indefinite pronouns are always singular: *anyone, each, every, everyone, nobody, no one, nothing, someone.*

These indefinite pronouns are always plural: *both, few, several, many.*

These indefinite pronouns depend on whether they are referring to one item (singular) or multiple items (plural): *all, any, enough, more, most, none, plenty, some.*

When two subjects are joined by *and*, they become plural. This mistake is easy to miss.

Chapter 3 Quiz

Reminder: write answers in shorthand.
1.) Name the three basic parts of the sentence:
2.) What is a sentence fragment?
3.) How can you tell if a sentence is in danger of being a run-on?
4.) When writing a sentence, what is important to ask yourself?
5.) What is the verb-subject agreement?
6.) Why is it important to get the verb-subject agreement correct?
7.) Does nor and or take singular or plural verbs?
8.) What are the three basic recommendations for the verb-subject agreement?
9.) Explain the problem with this sentence:

Since Larry enjoys driving, the forklift is the ideal job for him.

10.) Why should you make people the subjects rather than inanimate objects?

11.) What does starting a sentence with there imply?

12.) What are four ways to spot a run-on sentence?

13.) Why are this and that bad subjects?

14.) Rewrite this sentence:

Here is a book that you will enjoy.

15.) When is it okay to put a subject after the verb?

4.

Subtle Techniques Within Sentences

15-minute read

This chapter concentrates on improving the words within sentences. Chapter 5 focuses on ways to improve entire paragraphs and the structure of the message itself. Without further ado, here are 19 techniques.

1. The active verb spaghetti sauce.

Creative writers strive for active verbs. Writers in the workplace seem to have trouble knowing what they are. Whenever you see *is, are, was* or *were*, look for a stronger verb.
Word search is a marvelous tool; use it to count the number of passive verbs. Did you use *is* 60 times in your 200-word blog? It is difficult to cut out all such verbs but try reducing them to say 30 times.
Count how many sentences you have. Try to have 30% to 60% using active verbs. By searching for *is* or *are*, we can see easy ways to improve the verb.
Remember this key point – don't turn every *is* or *are* or *was* or *were* into an active verb. It makes writing awkward and the author looks like he or she is trying way too hard. It's like making a secret

spaghetti sauce -- you don't want to add every herb from your cabinet.

2. Dangling modifiers are one of the greatest dangers in writing.

They modify the wrong words, thus leaving the reader confused. You can teach yourself to look for dangling modifiers. Here are crucial hints: Seek words ending in *-ed* or *-ing* and acting as adjectives.

Running along the lake, the trees provided me with shade.

It'd be quite a sight to see running trees. A simple rewrite:

The trees provided shade when I ran along the lake.

Another example:

Educated as an engineer, the project looked easy to him.

It'd be quite a sight to see an educated project. A simple rewrite:

The project looked easy to him because he was educated as an engineer.

3. Avoid adjectives or adverbs.

Bloomberg News founder Matt Winkler instituted this rule when he began the news service. Incoming reporters and editors often chafed, but we either obeyed or went to work for the lower-paying daily newspapers. It will help your writing once you understand the reasoning. For example, look at this adjective:

John is a skinny man.

Skinny is subjective and open to interpretation. Think of more description in your sentence:

John weighs 150 pounds and stands 6 feet, 2 inches tall.

You the writer are showing that John is indeed skinny.

The elimination of adjectives and adverbs forces a writer to become more precise. Notice the difference between these two sentences:

Her Asian background makes her an asset to our company.
Her ability to speak Mandarin makes her an asset to our company.

"Most adjectives are unnecessary," writes William Zinsser in his great book, On Writing Well. "Like adverbs, they are sprinkled into sentences by writers who don't stop to think that the concept is already in the noun."

Zinsser points out examples -- yellow daffodils, very unique and brownish dirt – where the adjectives are stating the obvious.

Like Zinsser, I am not opposed to all adjectives and adverbs. If you limit them, they will become more vivid when they appear. Make them count.

4. Prepositional phrases are multi-word versions of adjectives and adverbs.

They may not modify the correct words and thus become dangling modifiers. These prepositions are the keys to spotting such phrases:

with
at
by
in

You can remember these prepositions by use of the acronym *wabi*.

Anytime you spot these prepositions, make sure they are modifying the right words. Learn to identify prepositional phrases and cut them out if not needed. Your main point may get lost in the clutter of other words.

5. By contrast with a prepositional phrase, a clause is a group of words with a subject and a verb.

There are several types that can be confusing such as independent clause, dependent clause, relative clause, etc.

Clauses have so many ticking time bombs. They are like the person who sticks his nose into every issue, complicating the point of the sentence.

The biggest problem is the clause may focus the reader on something that isn't the main point of the sentence. For example:

The main concerns of the workers, who enjoy their days off on Mondays and Tuesdays, are their pay raises.

Here, the clause about enjoying days off muddles the main point that workers are concerned about their pay raises. A simple rewrite:

The workers are most concerned about their pay raises.

These words are signals of clauses:

who
although
that
which
if
because
after

Call it the acronym *watwiba*.

BTW, I just invented these acronyms *wabi* and *watwiba* to help you remember the words to identify phrases and clauses. I find inventing acronyms to be a good way to remember a long list of words and explain this technique further in Chapter 5.

When you see a clause, look carefully. Readers will usually believe the clause is discussing the noun immediately preceding it.

Professional writers and their editors work to make sure the clause modifies the right word.

Since writing isn't your occupation, a simple technique is to make the clause modify the noun immediately preceding it.

The risk of avoiding clauses is that writers and lovers of reading might call your writing simple. Some people love dissecting long sentences to find out what the author really meant. However, we are writing for people in business. We want readers to immediately understand. Just think of all the unread and unloved thesis papers in schools around the world.

As discussed in Chapter 3, try to aim for one idea per sentence and maybe a clause or modifier. If you want a combination of both short and long sentences, try a pattern of one long sentence between two short sentences. When you review your first draft, the pattern will become more apparent.

6. What's an excellent way to spot clauses or phrases? Find the commas.

In grammar, the question is whether the clause is restrictive, i.e. needed, or non-restrictive, not needed. One big clue is that if the clause is restrictive, commas aren't needed.

Ask yourself – will this sentence make sense without the clause? If so, insert commas.

The greenhouse that was destroyed in the tornado is being re-built.
The greenhouse, which was destroyed in the tornado, is being re-built.

If you want to emphasize the tornado, skip the commas.

If you don't want to emphasize the tornado, the sentence can stand alone without it:

The greenhouse is being re-built.

Here are more examples:

People who live in glass houses shouldn't throw stones.

A short guide on how to write at work

People, who live in glass houses, shouldn't throw stones.

Commas are important when you have a name.

My brother, Bob, won the lottery.
My brother Bob won the lottery.

If Bob is needed in the sentence, don't use commas. Make it a restrictive clause.

7. Commas make the readers pause.

Try to avoid commas unless you want to highlight something.

The football, located in a spare locker, was flat.
The football located in a spare locker was flat.

The first sentence with commas focuses the readers' attention on located in a *spare locker* more than the word *flat*.

The second sentence doesn't cause the reader to pause, and the emphasis is on *flat*. Ask yourself which of these two do you want to emphasize?

It is always difficult to use clauses. Don't try to cram too much into a sentence. Use one idea per sentence, maybe two or three.

If you must use a clause, decide whether it is a necessary part of the sentence, or the sentence would be fine without it. Some commas are necessary, such as one after however. Look at these two sentences:

However Sharon thinks, the cat is dead.
However, Sharon thinks the cat is dead.

In the first sentence, the writer is saying Sharon's opinion doesn't matter. In the second sentence, the writer is saying what Sharon thinks.

Some believe that however shouldn't lead a sentence and instead should be used to connect separate ideas.

However, if these adverbs are placed elsewhere in the sentence, they can mess up the meaning of prior sentences.

There are so many rules for clauses that they will drive you nuts and distract you from the main purpose of your message. Still, it's good to know a few. Here are four rules from Strunk and White's Elements of Style:

-Enclose parenthetic expressions between commas
-Place a comma before a conjunction introducing an independent clause.
-Do not join independent clauses with a comma.
-Use a colon after an independent clause to introduce a list of particulars, an appositive, an amplification or an illustrative question.

Professional editors remember these rules because that is what they do for a living. If you practice these rules, you will learn them. If in doubt, give the clause in question a subject and verb and make it a second sentence.

9. Words to avoid:

a.) very – As writers, we use very to validate a point.

A short guide on how to write at work

> *This is very serious. I am very happy. She is very sad.*

Ask yourself – can this sentence do without very?

b.) really

> *This is really serious. I am really happy. She is really sad.*

Again, can the sentence really do without really? Really?

10. *But* was banned at Bloomberg when Matt Winkler was the editor in charge.
Reporters and editors who used but were dinged. Winkler's point is the sentence contained contradictory ideas. It leads to the *yes, but* sentence structure, which can lead to confusion.

> *I caught the ball, but I spilled my drink.*
> *She is a nice person, but she can be mean.*
> *The politician voted for the war, but he later turned against it.*

Daily newspaper reporters use this technique way too often. The next time you read an article, see if there is a *yes, but* construction. If there is, it's a signal that the story is poorly written. When you read an article, have a contest to see how *buts* are in the article. I was enjoying an article in my local paper, the Orange County Register, about a new restaurant when I read this sentence:

> *I think the term chef-driven gets used a lot when it's not the case, but here's it's absolutely true.*

It took me a while to comprehend what the writer was saying. How would I have rewritten it? I would have paraphrased it. Not every quote is perfect.

The chef sets the tone for what happens at the restaurant, he said.

I dropped chef-driven because the author said it's used too much! If that's the case, don't use it! It didn't add much and more importantly, I wanted the sentence to be clear to the reader. A writer cannot put every nuance into every article. If you find yourself in need of using but, try to rewrite the sentence or turn it into two sentences.

I caught the ball, and in the process, I spilled my drink.
She is a nice person. At times, she can be mean.
The politician voted for the war. Later, he turned against it.

But is a word that alerts readers a shift is occurring. Here are other shift signals:

Nonetheless
However
Still

These words are effective for transitions to new topics. There is no hard and fast rule on how many of these shift words to have. A guideline is to limit them to one or two per story.

PRO TIP 9: Do a search of your document. If you find too many words like nonetheless, however or still, you are pulling your reader in too many directions and giving too many options.

11. A dash is considered sophomoric by some critics.

I rather like dashes because they can help you out of a tight spot. Take this sentence from an article that I was editing while working as a contract writer at Pimco, one of the world's largest bond investors.

The three components of TIPS yield, BBB credit spread and equity risk premium (a function of the S&P 500 forward earnings yield), are shown in the solid bars.

Even if you know the meaning of TIPS yield and credit spreads, this sentence is difficult to understand. Any reader would pause at this sentence to figure out what exactly is being said.
Ask yourself why it is hard to understand? Because the subject is so far from the verb – 19 words separate them. A fellow editor suggested an elegant solution – the addition of dashes to make the subject appear much closer to the verb.

The three components – TIPS yield, BBB credit spread and equity risk premium (a function of the S&P 500 forward earnings yield) – are shown in the solid bars.

12. Parallelism is when things are listed in a sentence and something is missing,

Parallelism isn't as widely feared as the dangling modifier or verb-subject agreement. When it doesn't work, the reader pauses and thinks, something is wrong here but cannot put his or her finger on it. Look at this sentence that I originally drafted for an article:

The bank said it "significantly re-positioned and de-risked the balance sheet" by reducing brokered deposits, reclassifying held-to-maturity securities as available for sale and sales of longer-duration, mortgage-backed securities.

I wanted to cram a lot of information into a short space. I used a present participle – reducing and reclassifying -- for the first two items in the list and a noun -- sales -- for the third item. While reviewing this sentence, I specifically looked for the parallelism and corrected it by merely changing sales to selling.

The bank said it "significantly re-positioned and de-risked the balance sheet" by reducing brokered deposits, reclassifying held-to-maturity securities as available for sale and selling longer-duration, mortgage-backed securities.

Here is an example of parallelism that doesn't work:

The football players were not only both big and fast, but they also were able to maintain running pace with the members of the track and basketball teams.

The sentence has the *yes but* construction, making it bounce like an incomplete pass. The parallelism is off. Try it this way:

Not only were the football players big and fast, they also were able to maintain running pace with the members of the track and basketball teams.

A nice technique is placing the verb or object closer to the subject and letting the preposition follow. For example:

She has been both critical of the actors and the writing.
She has been critical of both the actors and the writing.

He neither caught the ball nor ran after it.
He caught neither the ball nor ran after it.

Parallelism can be spotted with the construction of sentences like *either ... or, neither... nor or both ... and .. but.*

13. Start a sentence with the older information and then move to the newer items.

Mary went to college after she finished high school.
After Mary finished high school, she went to college.

This helps the reader go through a historical progression of what is happening by moving from left to right.
One exception is numbers. Look at these two sentences.

Our revenue climbed from $80 million to $90 million.
Our revenue climbed to $90 million from $80 million.

At Bloomberg, our style was the latter. At first, it felt awkward, but then it made more sense. The first number mentioned is the news and is more easily remembered. In this first example, $80 million

47

stands out while $90 million is more prominent in the second example.
Go with the news.

14. These adverbs are landmines that can blow up the meaning of your sentences.

also
only
not
however

Generally, these adverbs should be placed before a verb and not a noun such as these examples.

I only think of you.
I also think of you.
However, I think of you.
I do not think of you.
If you want to play around, try placing them elsewhere:
I think of only you.
I think of also you.
I think of you, however.
Not that I think of you.

The problems start when the sentences get longer, and the words are misplaced. Look at how the meaning of each sentence is changed:

I only think of you when I am driving the truck.
I think of you only when I am driving the truck.
I think of you when I am only driving the truck.

I also think of you when I am driving the truck.
I think of also you when I am driving the truck.
I think of you when I am also driving the truck.

However, I think of you when I am driving the truck.
I think of you when, however, I am driving the truck.
I think of you when I am driving the truck, however.

I do not think of you.
Not that I think of you.
I think not of you.

Each sentence carries a different meaning. When you see these four adverbs – only, also, however, not – carefully review the sentence to see if the adverb is modifying the correct verb.

15. Avoid the double negative. It makes the reader stop and think about what was said.

It's impossible to not like him.

Instead:

Everyone likes him.

PRO TIP 10: Some elite colleges teach the double negative as a delightful way to be snobbish and the leaving the intended victim unaware of the condescension. Here, famous double negatives from Groucho Marx leave the listener wondering what was truly meant:

I cannot say that I do not disagree with you.
He was not incompetent.
She is not unattractive.

49

16. When you see these words begin sentences, they signal a clause is beginning a sentence. Consider rewriting the sentence.

as
like
unlike

17. Avoid roller coasters in the same sentence: *over and under, underlying, overcoming, over, emphasis, internal, underlines, over, long run, short-term.*

Bob ran over the cat while driving under the bridge.

18. Said is a perfectly fine attribution.

It may look boring to constantly use it, but using other attributions carry meanings that you may not intend. Take this sentence for example:

"Our competitors have inferior products," he claimed.

The definition of *claim* as a verb is: asserting something is the case without providing proof.
Experienced journalists may use claimed as a coded word to imply the statement may be false.

"Our competitors have inferior products," he stated.

Stated implies that this is a fact rather than an opinion. Using the word stated also leaves the impression he is speaking in a courtroom or before a group of diplomats.

A short guide on how to write at work

"Our competitors have inferior products," he grinned.

A reader might ask, what is he grinning about? Is this guy a smart ass? The reader then focuses on the grin rather than the main point.

"Our competitors have inferior products," he said.

Here is where the reader passes over said to concentrate on the speaker's main point – competitors have inferior products.

19. *You* is a preachy word.

You did this, *you* did that. Why don't *you* do this?

I used *you* too many times in one of my first columns as a reporter at my college paper. My instructor pointed out that *you* is preachy. She was write. A writer should avoid sounding like a preacher. Instead, use the passive voice or the plural we to make you and the recipient appear that you are both striving for the same goal. Which one of these sounds best?

You are not correctly installing the curtains.
The curtains aren't correctly installed.
We need to correctly install the curtains.

20. The exclamation mark!!!

Professional writers seldom use exclamation marks, which are signs of someone trying too hard. It's like a cheerleader passionately cheering when her basketball team is 50 points behind and clearly going to lose.

I'm not against all exclamation marks. I remember once using an exclamation mark in a quote in a press release only to be told by my PR supervisor that she never uses them and she quickly excised the demon.

To each his own. There's no set guideline on how often to use them. My advice is to use an exclamation mark sparingly, maybe once every 10 writings. If you add an exclamation mark every other sentence, it is distracting to the eye and the narrative.

Chapter 4 Quiz
Reminder: write answers in shorthand.

1.) What is the difference between active and passive verbs?

2.) What is a clue to finding a passive verb?

3.) What's the problem with making every verb active?

4.) Find the problem in this sentence:

When jogging on New York City streets, the buildings are fabulous to look at.

5.) What is good advice on adjectives and adverbs in business writing? Why?

6.) What is the problem with clauses?

7.) What are the seven signs of clauses?

8.) When you see a clause, what should you look for?

9.) What's an excellent way to spot clauses or phrases?

10.) What do commas cause the reader to do?

11.) What are two words to always avoid because they are unnecessary?

12.) What is the problem with but?

13.) What is the problem with too much usage of words like nonetheless, however or still.

14.) Describe parallelism.

15.) What is a common technique to describe the history of something?

16.) What is a double negative?

17.) When these words start a sentence, what do they indicate?

18.) What words indicate a sentence is a roller coaster?

19.) What does claim infer?

20.) Why avoid the use of you when writing?

21.) What does an exclamation mark signal?

5.

Beyond Sentences

15-minute read

Now that we've learned techniques inside of a sentence, let's take a wider approach to writing. Here are 14 techniques followed by writers and editors.

1. The two biggest secrets to creative writing are characters and tension.

Every single book or movie has these two elements. Who can forget Hans Solo and Darth Vader? They are interesting characters. There is tension between them and the others. The readers or viewers want to know what happens to these characters and how they resolve their problems.

Now for the good news. Since writing for business isn't creative writing, we don't have to focus on interesting characters or creating tension. However, we can use these two elements to our advantage.

Tension is inherent in business. Employers know if they don't satisfy customers, sales are not made. Employees know if they don't do their jobs, they are fired or demoted.

We can add tension by pointing out a problem and then recommending possible solutions.

A short guide on how to write at work

Sales of the R Widgets are not meeting expectations. We can try placing them in new locations in the stores, reducing the price by a few percentage points or asking employees to promote them to customers. I'm open to other suggestions.

We can highlight the achievements of employees in an email or a blog. For example, let's think of ways to improve the following sentence about Bob:

Bob is a standout employee for us.

This is a generic compliment. Ask yourself, how is Bob a standout employee? What do you remember that makes you think this? Note an example of what you like about Bob.

Bob is a standout employee who always has a pleasant smile and a welcoming hello.

or

Bob is a standout employee who helps his colleagues succeed in their jobs.

Now, tell a personal detail about Bob:

Bob is a standout employee who helps his colleagues succeed in their jobs. In his spare time, he likes to go golfing with his 85-year-old father.

Readers will think that Bob is a good son to spend time with his father. The sentence implies that since Dad is still golfing at 85, he must be in good shape. It's a compliment enjoyed by everyone. With a few extra words, you have created goodwill.

PRO TIP 11: Everyone loves seeing their name in print in a good way. If you have a chance to mention someone in writing, do so. And if possible, mention their spouses or children or other relatives you have met. Double-check that you've correctly spelled the names.

2. The first sentence of your message is your prime real estate.

Don't block the view of your readers. Don't clutter the first sentence with a clause or a phrase or extra words. I recently edited the lead of a sentence similar to this:

Integrity, persistence and courage helped John Doe overcome obstacles.

Note the problem. The first four words are the subject of the sentence. Worse, they are generic and easily forgettable. In the first sentence, don't use a list or the words *but, or*, or *and.*

PRO TIP 12: Try to avoid all commas in your first sentence because they indicate a clause that will take away from your main point.

Most speech givers know a subtle technique – don't say anything important in the first 30 seconds or so. The crowd is getting used to you and is looking at your clothes, the surroundings and not paying as much attention. The listeners will stay at least a few minutes.

Writing is different. We must attract the readers' attention immediately. The audience is familiar with the setting for the written word. Get right to it. Or they will stop reading your message or story.

PRO TIP 13: If your first sentence is longer than 16 words, consider rewriting it. Just one subject, one verb and one object.

3. Use short words instead of many syllables.

Ignore the intellectuals who criticize journalists for writing at the level of eighth graders.

Journalists write for a living and that means seeking a broad audience. Their practices have been sharpened in the eyes of the public for hundreds of years. If their writing isn't understood, they go out of business. Writing well for business means not causing the reader to ponder for days about what was really meant.

Great writing can be with short words. Lincoln's 2nd inaugural address used 701 words, 505 one syllable and 122 words of two syllables.

4. The wonders of a template.

When an old-time journalist heard of a fire or another catastrophe, he would pull a template out of his drawer and just fill in the who, what, when, where and why. When I heard this story as a young journalism student, I was appalled. I felt that every story should be like an original painting.

I'm wiser now. Templates organize your thoughts and save time. They are just the kick starter to a story.

In fact, everyone in journalism uses templates. Here is a typical template that the Wall Street Journal made famous and the rest of the media copies with middling results:

For classes, private lessons: Howtowriteatwork@gmail.com

a.) First two to four paragraphs begin with an example of an issue – also known as anecdote.

b.) The fourth or fifth paragraph is what is called "nut graph" where the importance of the issue is explained.

c.) Statistics are cited.

d.) Contrary opinions are provided to bring drama and tension into the story.

e.) One or two more examples of statistics are given.

f.) More commentary is provided to prove the beginning anecdote.

g.) Ending comment.

Consider building a template of these forms:

E-mails.
Blogs.
Sponsored content.
Thought leadership papers.
White papers.

5. The four horsemen: If you're writing a thought leadership or white paper, here are four types to consider, according to Amy Einsohn in The Copyeditor's Handbook:

a.) Compare and contrast
b.) Observations and predictions
c.) Problem and solution
d.) Argument – proposes a thesis, presents data or reasons, disposes of counter-arguments.

6. Euphemisms can sometimes be helpful to executives.

As a journalist, I've read many press releases where a company says it is laying off employees. My editors would say, "Cut through the bullshit. Unless those employees are being re-hired, we report they are being fired."

The harshness of these words didn't bother me because we journalists are tough as nails and not willing to hide the truth from our readers.

After I was "fired" as part of a group of 90 journalists let go at Bloomberg News, I saw the benefit of trying to soften the blow for employees.

When it's one executive who is dismissed, the euphemism is the person is spending more time with his or her family. It's much a better way to treat an employee who spent so much time at your company.

For executives writing from the perspective of the company, there's a need to soften the blow. Don't go overboard. For example, I have read press releases that say an executive in his 40s is retiring. That is a company hiding what is happening.

7. Know your audience. If you are writing for a particular industry, use the words of that industry. If you are writing for someone outside the industry, make it simple, something your mother or father could understand.

This is easier said than done. Jargon is the term for words used in an industry that outsiders have a difficult time understanding. Journalists are taught to avoid jargon by writing to as wide an audience as possible.

In my view, it's important to understand your audience. I've read thousands of reports by analysts describing publicly traded companies that they cover. A reader who doesn't understand stocks or that industry would be as lost as a tourist in the jungle.

However, the readers who are investors know well the jargon. If these analysts avoided the jargon, they might give the impression they don't know well the industry. The audience for these analyst reports understands the jargon and appreciates it to reduce word count and explanations.

This is where it's important to understand your readers. If they understand your jargon, feel free to use such words. Consider this sentence:

The bank's NIM widened to a record in Q4, according to the 10Q that was released on EDGAR.

The sentence contains four words that are jargon: NIM, Q4, 10Q, EDGAR. A banking executive would understand the sentence. If the reader is not in the banking industry, the sentence is confusing. String together three or more sentences like this and you've lost the non-banking audience. If your audience is wider than banking executives, get rid of the jargon words:

The bank's net interest margin, a key gauge of profitability, widened to a record in the fourth quarter, according to a quarterly filing with the Securities and Exchange Commission electronic database called EDGAR.

8. Avoid asking questions that provide a yes or no answer.

Don't ask:

Did you go to the warehouse yesterday?

Instead, ask why or how questions:

Why did you go or not go to the warehouse yesterday?

9. Quotes enliven any story.

Corporate press releases botch quotes all the time. Look at this actual quote in a 2017 press release from IBM:

"Digitization, Internet of Things, global connectivity and the integration of new disruptive technologies are some megatrends opening a lot of new business opportunities. However, they also bring new threats with possible high impact on the industry. We operate the infrastructure of the Swiss financial market. IBM as leading company in Security Operations and Response was the logical partner for us and the perfect match for our requirements to build and operate our SIX Security Operations Center which will go beyond today's off-the-shelf cyber security standards – therefore defining the next generation of the Swiss financial market", says Robert Bornträger, Division CEO SIX Global IT.

That quote is 103 words. Egads – how many people can get through that quote?
Let's improve it in a couple of ways. First, the subject of the first sentence in a quote shouldn't be a list. Make a new subject.
Replace some with important because the speaker has

obviously thought about which examples to highlight and in that speaker's view, they are not merely some.

Don't cite examples if you don't consider them the important ones. Then we'll add the attribution after the first sentence, rather than leaving it to the last part. Next, we'll break this long paragraph into two.

"The important megatrends for new business opportunities are digitization, the Internet of Things, global connectivity and the integration of new disruptive technologies," said Robert Bornträger, Division CEO SIX Global IT, which operates the infrastructure of the Swiss financial market. "However, they also bring new threats with possible high impact on the industry.

"IBM as the leading company in Security Operations and Response was the logical partner for us and the perfect match for our requirements to build and operate our SIX Security Operations Center," Bornträger said. "This center will go beyond today's off-the-shelf cyber security standards – therefore defining the next generation of the Swiss financial market."

While the quotes are longer at 106 words, they are much more readable.

Another technique for quotes -- don't start with the attribution. Try to read this actual quote:

Patrick Yam, CEO and Co-Founder of Somnology Inc., the premier enterprise in the illumination and monitoring of sleep disorders states: "We're pleased to announce today's collaboration with a leading national medical institute, The National Institute of Health (NIH). Recognizing the accuracy of Somnology's digital healthcare device the Plex®

A short guide on how to write at work

Sleep Scanner and, the paramount importance of monitoring sleep for disorders we look forward to establishing a successful working relationship. Our collaboration reflects a profound comprehension among leading medical authorities that sleep disorders are an adversarial catalyst accentuating co-morbidities as obesity, Alzheimer's, Diabetes, cardiac-related diseases and other health maladies.

The reader must wade through 20 words before getting to the beginning of the quote. That is like a hotel builder putting a bathroom where the view should be.

To make quotes readable, place the attribution *said* after the first sentence to help the reader understand the most important part of the quote first and then quickly know who is speaking. Don't wait to place *said* at the end of two or more sentences.

Try to save a quote for interesting comments. The previous quote leads with a generic remark that can be paraphrased. We can break this paragraph into two and make the quote far more interesting by reorganizing it to place the prime issue – sleep disorders – in the front of the paragraph.

Somnology Inc., the premier enterprise in the illumination and monitoring of sleep disorders, is pleased to announce a collaboration with the National Institute of Health (NIH), one of the nation's top medical institutes.

"Our collaboration reflects a profound comprehension among leading medical authorities that sleep disorders are an adversarial catalyst accentuating co-morbidities as obesity, Alzheimer's, Diabetes, cardiac related diseases and other health maladies," Patrick Yam, CEO and Co-Founder of

Somnology, said. "The National Institute recognizes the accuracy of Somnology's digital healthcare device the Plex Sleep Scanner and, the paramount importance of monitoring sleep for disorders."

Also, note that *said* is after the subject. Only place *said* before the subject if there is a long title between the two.

10. Lists are popular.

Readers love them so the media provides more of them. Who wouldn't want to read this story?

Five ways to become a millionaire

Lists have their own idiosyncrasies. Let's break it down on how to create them. First, a list in a sentence can put readers to sleep:

The requirements include agility, knowledge, honesty, intelligence and speed.

Newspaper reporters and editors are trained to keep the list to three items to retain the attention of the readers. The first and last items are likely to be remembered, but less so for the items in the middle of knowledge, honesty and intelligence. If you're going to write a list, put only three items. More than three will be forgotten.

The requirements include knowledge, honesty and speed.

A short guide on how to write at work

Start with the shortest word first and keep the longest word or phrase to the last. Ask yourself which is easier to read:

Our product comes in pink polka-dots, blue and red.

or

Our product comes in red, blue and pink polka-dots.

Begin the list with the subject. Take this sentence,

Thick thigh muscles, hand strength, speed, quickness and toughness are required by us for good running backs.

The first problem is that the list starts the sentence and what should be the subject, *us,* is the object. Let's turn that around so the subject appears before the list.

We require good running backs to have thick thigh muscles, hand strength, speed, quickness and toughness.

Still, readers tend to gloss over such lists and words like speed are missed.

The reason journalists and newspapers write this way is that newsprint was expensive. We had to be frugal. We listed the requirements as quickly and economically as we could. These days of the Internet, we have much more space. Ironically, with more people reading on their narrow cell phones, paragraphs with more than two sentences look much longer – the same as in the old days of narrow newspaper columns!

Because we have more space, we can have more fun than in the days when the cost of print kept down the amount of writing. Experiment with this sentence in a vertical list:

We require good running backs to have:
-Thick thigh muscles
-Hand strength
-Speed
-Quickness
-Toughness

Then the writer may emphasize details of each requirement:

--Thick thigh muscles to help the player keep moving when tackled
--Hand strength to hold onto the football
--Speed to run a 40-yard dash below 6 seconds
--Quickness to shift suddenly to the left or right
--Toughness to get up after being tackled

Look at this sentence:

It's important that our customers receive great products, excellent service, accuracy and honesty.

Our eyes tend to glaze over such lists. Studies have shown that the middle items tend to be ignored and the first and last items are remembered. Try it this way:

It's important that our customers receive:
Great products
Excellent service
Accuracy
Trustworthiness

11. Acronyms are often boring, particularly when used by governments.

How many people know that CalSTRS is the California government pension system or that the NCUA is the National Credit Union Administrator?

Still, we can have fun by turning a boring sentence into our own acronym.

For example, the investment world was struggling to explain that only four stocks were driving the Nasdaq higher: Netflix, Google, Facebook and Apple.

CNBC business host Jim Cramer was witty enough to turn this into an acronym: FANG for Facebook, Amazon, Netflix and Google.

It worked wonders as commentators in newspapers or on television could use this as a shorthand way to explain what the market was doing.

Look at this ordinary sentence:

It's important that our customers receive great products, excellent service, accuracy and honesty.

Let's build an acronym that people will remember. Start by picking a word that you want people to remember. This is where writing becomes fun. Say you like the word tiger because it's an animal that is tough and beautiful. So, spell it vertically:

T
I
G
E
R

Let's look at Thesaurus.com for synonyms that start with T:

T – Tremendous can be an acronym for great.

What starts with I? Integrity is a nice synonym of honesty. And so we continue:

G – Great effort.
E – Excellent service.
R – Rewarding

Which sentence would you remember?

It's important that our customers receive great products, excellent service, accuracy and honesty.

> *Team, we must embrace the Tiger Principle:*
> *T – Tremendous product that we believe in.*
> *I -- Integrity. No need to lie or exaggerate what we sell.*
> *G – Great Effort*
> *E – Excellent Service. Answer any and every question customers have.*
> *R – Reward -- a commission for your sales.*

Say you are writing a webpage to describe the history of your company. You can do it two ways:

Start with the oldest information on top and then cascade down to the newest.

Or

Start with the newest information and go backward in history.

Let's see how this works using First National Bank as an example:

1874: Founded in Omaha, Nebraska.
1882: Opens branch in Kansas City, Missouri
1905: Starts brokerage to trade commodities.
1929: Prepares for Great Depression.
1939: Starts issuing U.S. Savings Bond
1955: Opens third branch in St. Louis
1961: Praised by President John F. Kennedy as an example of great lending practices.
1971: Buys Third National Bank to double its assets.
1997: Begins offering online banking.
2005: Provide end-to-end mortgage services online.
2008: Avoids 2008 financial crisis with sound lending practices.
2010: Permits customers to deposit checks using their cell phones.
2013: Acquires the assets of Fifth National Bank to become the largest bank in the Midwest.
2017: Provides highest interest rate for certificates of deposit in the Midwest.

Notice what the problem is? It's what we call in the media: Burying your lead. The oldest news is on top and the newest news is on the bottom. How many customers will read all the way to the bottom. I recommend starting with the newest and then go down to the oldest. Let's switch this around:

2017: Provides highest interest rate for certificates of deposit in the Midwest.
2013: Acquires the assets of Fifth National Bank to become the largest bank in the Midwest.
2010: Permits customers to deposit checks using

their cell phones.
2008: Avoids 2008 financial crisis with sound
lending practices.
2005: Provide end-to-end mortgage services
online.
1997: Begins offering online banking.
1971: Buys Third National Bank to double its
assets.
1961: Praised by President John F. Kennedy as an
example of great lending practices.
1955: Opens third branch in St. Louis
1939: Starts issuing U.S. Savings Bond
1929: Prepares for Great Depression.
1905: Starts brokerage to trade commodities.
1882: Opens branch in Kansas City, Missouri
1874: Founded in Omaha, Nebraska.

12. Who likes being criticized?

Nobody, but sometimes bosses must correct what they see as mistakes by their employees.
The best way, when possible, is one-on-one. But sometimes a problem is widespread. In these cases:

-- Compliment the group on something they did well.
-- Say you noticed there are areas that can be improved and explain what you want to happen.
-- End with another compliment.

For example, say the office kitchen is a pigsty. An office manager sent out an email like this:

The kitchen is a disgrace with crumbs and leftover
food all over the place. Keep it clean!

A short guide on how to write at work

A typical employee may think he didn't make the mess so it doesn't apply to him and besides, the boss doesn't pay enough or give enough time to go to lunch. Instead, a boss might send a message like:

I'm happy to see everyone loves the convenience of the office kitchen.
I would like to point out that I sometimes see a mess in the kitchen. Please clean up after yourself so other people can use a clean kitchen.
It's nice to see people eating healthy food and talking to each other in the kitchen.

The above example uses a conditional verb that softly advises what you want to happen. In cases like this, the conditional is better than the active verb that is a command.

13. To paraphrase an old saying: What do opinions and assholes have in common? Everyone has one.

When we write, it's easy to give our opinions about something. Some people may listen. Others may not. Furthermore, when we write about areas where we don't have the expertise, say the political scandal of the day, we may miss a nuance that we regret. This nuance is often why executives at corporations avoid making political statements.

Professional writers are paid to be controversial and get attention. Plus, like lawyers, they have subtle techniques to cover their asses if the controversy becomes too big.

What's more interesting is to write about the opinions of others. Say you are an executive who wants to praise a department in your weekly message. You write the following:

Congrats to the shipping department for its excellent job.

How do you liven it up so people remember this comment?

Don't look for active verbs. Look for people to include.

Ask the executive in charge of that department or one of its employees why that department is doing so well as to merit your praise. Include their names in your writing.

Congrats to the shipping department for its excellent job. Bob Jones tells me that Mary always double-checks that the right products are in the correct box and Andy is an expert at making sure the address is correct.

Active verbs are not the key – names are. Successful business writing includes other people. Everyone likes to be cited in a favorable way.

An employee can show this message to his co-workers or family or bosses. Such compliments in the workplace are far more important than a fancy turn of a phrase.

Whereas the first message was generic, the second message will please five people, including Chief Bob Jones who can impress on his employees that he is telling management about the good job they are doing. Always try to get the opinions of others into your messages. This technique is far better than your own opinion.

14. The Four Paragraphs:

A short guide on how to write at work

The Elements of Style's Workbook says there are four types of paragraphs:

a.) Expository – the writer explains something
b.) Narrative – the writer tells what happened, usually in chronological order
c.) Descriptive – the writer describes something
d.) Persuasive – the writer persuades the reader of a viewpoint.

Politicians nowadays talk about controlling the narrative. By that, they mean getting the media to mention only the most favorable parts to the politicians and leaving out sections that damage them.

The business writer doesn't need to be so cynical. Simply determine which of these four types of paragraphs you are writing and go to it.

The Quiz

Reminder: write answers in shorthand.

1.) What are the two biggest secrets to creative writing?

2.) How do you add tension to business writing?

3.) Make this sentence more interesting:
Bob is a standout employee.

4.) What should you always doublecheck the spelling of?

5.) What is prime real estate in writing?

6.) What should you avoid in your first sentence and why?

7.) How many words should your first sentence be under?

8.) How many words were in Lincoln's 2nd inaugural address?

9.) What is the benefit of a template?

10.) Where can templates be used?

11.) What are four types to consider for thought leadership or white paper?

12.) What do you think when you read an executive in his or her 40s is leaving the company to retire?

13.) What is the importance of knowing who will read what you write?

14.) Trim this quote from a press release:

"Digitization, Internet of Things, global connectivity and the integration of new disruptive technologies are some megatrends opening a lot of new business opportunities. However, they also bring new threats with possible high impact on the industry. We operate the infrastructure of the Swiss financial market. IBM as leading company in Security Operations and Response was the logical partner for us and the perfect match for our requirements to build and operate our SIX Security Operations Center which will go beyond today's off-the-shelf cyber security standards – therefore defining the next generation of the Swiss financial market", says Robert Bornträger, Division CEO SIX Global IT.

15.) What is wrong with starting a quote with an attribution?

16.) Why are lists popular?

17.) If you're going to list items in a sentence, how many items should you list?

18.) When you list things, where should the longest item be?

19.) What are the problems with acronyms?

20.) How can you build an interesting acronym?

21.) When you build a timeline, should it be oldest to newest or newest to last? Why?

22.) How do you write a sentence that criticizes a person or group?

23.) Why are opinions like assholes?

A short guide on how to write at work

24.) How would you liven up this sentence?
Congrats to the shipping department for its excellent
job.
25.) Name the four types of paragraphs:

6.

Confusing Words

15-minute read

To speak well, don't speak good. Many people violate this rule, to their own detriment. For example:

He runs very good.

Good is an adjective that should modify a noun. Here it modifies a verb, so it should be the adverb well:

He runs very well.

In colloquial English, good is often misused in place of well. Athletes and actors are infamous for the incorrect use of English. To confuse the issue a bit, well can sometimes be used as an adjective in addition to an adverb. But good is never used as an adverb.

Words are misused all the time. As a kid growing up in Hawaii, the correct use of language was no big thing bro. But as I've grown older and wiser, I notice people will judge you on how you speak.

Nowadays, I often hear one of my favorite radio talk show hosts misuse the word *literally* when he means *figuratively*.

A short guide on how to write at work

When I hear that, I don't want to *literally* strangle him but rather *figuratively* strangle him.
People get promoted because the boss thinks they are smart. If you cannot remember this simple good/well rule, the boss may think not. If you use words incorrectly, it's a shorthand way for people to judge your intelligence.

We can also use this to our own advantage by determining if the person speaking is intelligent enough to realize the correct use of words.
In this chapter, I feature words that I have to remind myself to use correctly. It's quite easy to miss them when typing. Spell Check won't catch the mistake either. I've witnessed programs like Grammarly miss some basic words.

The following is divided into two sections.

A.) Section 1 features the words that I have found most often misused during my 40 years of journalism.

B.) Second II provides other words that are often misused and good to know, but not as obvious a mistake.

These are words that I myself have sometimes botched. If you can remember them, editors will think you are a good writer.

The words are in alphabetical order to help you find them quickly when you return to this chapter. Print out this chapter and have it at your side when writing.

Section 1:

accept
except
Spelling programs won't catch this obvious mistake.

For classes, private lessons: Howtowriteatwork@gmail.com

advice: the noun
advise: the verb

affect: verb to make something happen. Examples:
The movie affected me.
The story affected the way I think.

effect: noun. Hint: Effect doesn't sound right as a verb.
> *The movie effected me.*
Try it this way:
> *The movie's special effects were fantastic.*

aid: verb to assist
aide: a noun that means helper

allusion: indirect reference to something like a secret treasure
delusion: idea without a basis in reality
illusion: a visual trick

Here are examples:
She alluded to an elephant in the jungle.
She was deluded into thinking she was an elephant in the jungle.
She thought she saw an elephant in the jungle, but it was an illusion.

ambiguous: vague, unclear
ambivalent: strong opposing feelings

assure: make a person comfortable
ensure: make sure something happens
insure: insurance policy

average: same as mean
mean: same as average

A short guide on how to write at work

median: the middle number in a range ordered from low to high.

Say you have the salaries of people in a movie. The screenwriter earned $50,000, the cameraman $40,000, the director $100,000, the assistant director $75,000 and the star $2 million. An average salary would be $453,000. That is misleading because only one person made more than that figure – the star, whose salary increased the average. Instead, the median salary of the person in the middle -- $75,000 – provides a more realistic interpretation of the salaries.

bear: the animal is the noun. Bear is used as a verb as in bear the burden
bare: naked. Hint. Ask yourself if this looks right: That woman is bear naked.

bring: moving towards the object
take: moving away from the object

censor: to prohibit the use of something
censer: container to burn incense
censure: condemn

choose: to pick out
chose: past tense of choose

compliment: admiration
complement: counterpart

condone: to approve with reluctance
condemn: to indicate unfavorable judgment

discreet: circumspect, not the obvious
discrete: separate, different

disinterested: unaffected by the results
uninterested: bored, uncaring of the effects

PRO TIP 14: Well-educated people pay attention to the difference in disinterested, which is unaffected, and uninterested, which is
uncaring.

Figuratively: Indicates imagination and didn't really happen
Literally: Indicates something that actually occurred, without exaggeration

hear: when you hear something.
here: where you are located

him, her, me, us, them: these are pronouns to use as objects.
I, he, she, it: Use as subject in the sentence.
When in doubt, try this technique: Insert the pronoun in place of a name. For example:

> *I gave the ball to George. (correct)*
> *Me gave the ball to George. (incorrect)*

> *He gave the ball to me (correct).*
> *He gave the ball to I (incorrect).*

> *Lisa and I went to the movies. (correct)*
> *Lisa and me went to the movies.*
> *(incorrect)*

> *The movie was attended by Lisa and me.*
> *(correct)*
> *The movie was attended by Lisa and I.*
> *(incorrect)*

A short guide on how to write at work

in: within
into: indicates movement towards the inside of
something.
in to: when adverb to is part of preposition to
Examples:

> *George's homework is in his briefcase.*
> *George turned his homework in to the*
> *teacher.*
> *George put his homework into his briefcase.*

incredulous: refers to people
incredible: refers to events

irregardless: never use – it's a double negative. It's
like the signal of well versus good,
regardless: always use

its: singular pronoun for an object that isn't human
it's: a contraction for it is. Examples:

> *Put the key in its proper place. (correct)*
> *Put the keys in its proper place. (incorrect –*
> *keys are plural so should be their).*
> *Put the key in it's proper place. (incorrect)*
> *It's a well-made key. (correct)*
> *Its a well-made key. (incorrect)*

lay: to put down, to place. It takes a direct object.
Hint: if you can use put, use lay.

> *I put this book on the table. I lay this book*
> *on the table.*

lie: to rest or recline (or to deceive).

> *I lie on the bed.*

Hint: If you try put here, it doesn't work: I put on the bed.

libel: to offend someone in a publication
slander: to offend someone by speaking

material: the substance of which a thing is made
materiel: military ordnance

personnel: employees
personal: private or close.
Hint: Which of these sentences sounds right?
> *This picture is personal.*
> *This picture is personnel.*

precede: verb that means to exist in a prior time.
Hint: it means before.
proceed: verb that means to go forward: Hint: carry on.
preceed: misspelling of the above two. Don't use at all!

principal: a person of authority. Hint: think of pal at the end as a person.
principle: an idea to follow

red: the color
read: reading a book
This seems way too obvious, but it's a common typo that automated word spelling won't catch.

stationery: writing paper
stationary: standing still

than: if can use "in comparison with," it is correct
then: if can use "next" instead, it is correct

that: usually a comma isn't needed.
which: usually comes after a comma
Hint: If a sentence needs a clause, use that. If the
sentence doesn't need the clause, use which.
Examples:
*The snow that piled up on the driveway prevented us
from leaving the house.*
*The snow, which piled up on the driveway, prevented
us from leaving the house.*

this and that: singular pronouns
these and those: plural pronouns

this and these: modify nouns nearby
that and those: modify nouns further away.

there: Nouns don't follow this but verbs do as in:
There is, there are
their: Nouns follow this such as their balls, their
boat.

threw: past tense of verb throw. He threw the ball.
through: proposition. in one side and out the other
thru: non-standard use of through; try to avoid
Which looks correct?
> *They walked threw the garden.*
> *They walked through the garden.*
> *She through the ball.*
> *She threw the ball.*

your: possessive as in *your book*
you're: a contraction of you are

who is, who are, who am: The verb that follows who
agrees with what the pronoun is replacing.
For example:

> *I am a doctor. Who is a doctor?*
> *We are doctors. Who are the doctors?*

very: usually modifies a verb. Some purists get upset when it modifies an adjective.
Best to avoid very because it is very over-used (pun intended!). Ask yourself – is it really needed in this sentence? Is there a difference if I take it out?

who vs. whom: There is a lot of confusion and debate on the proper way to use it.
Who should be used when referring to the subject.
Whom should be used when referring to the verb or the object.
Two simple tests can help. If you can
replace he or she or they, use who. If you use him or her, use whom.
Another simple way to remember is that when following a preposition, use whom.

> *To whom does this concern?*
> *Joey, from whom we get our apples, is a nice lad.*

you and I: Use as the subject of the sentence.
> *You and I are going to catch this wave.*

you and me: Use as the object of the sentence.
Hint: *The wave came to you and me.*
2nd hint: between you and me (not between you and I**)**

Section 2:
The second section will provide other words that are often misused and good to know, but not as obvious a mistake.

adverse: unfavorable

A short guide on how to write at work

averse: reluctant, opposed

all ready: preparation
already: has already occurred.

aloud
out loud: Less polished version of aloud.

among: more than two items.
between: for two items

capital: wealth
capitol: headquarters of a government

can: informal
may: politer version of can

cite: verb to reference a paper or article
site: noun meaning place

comprise: to include or be made up of
compose: consisting
compared to: use when making a comparison of different things
compared with: use when making a comparison of similar things

conscious: awake
conscientious: scrupulous, careful

continuous: implies unbroken sequence – river flow continuously
continual: series of discrete events: a day's work may suffer continual interruption

council: advisory group
counsel: to provide advice (lawyer)

due to: caused by
owing to: because of
flaunt: brag
flout: to treat with disdain

forego: to go before
forgo: to abstain

fortuitous: by chance or accident, either good or bad
fortunate: lucky

historic: momentous in history
historical: anything that occurred in the past.

if: conditional.
For example: Call if you can come -- means to call if you can come.
whether: to introduce an alternative. For example: Call whether you can come -- means to call regardless of the answer.

infer: draw a conclusion
imply: hint

naval: navy
navel: bellybutton

palate: taste, also the roof of a mouth
palette: artist's paint board
pallet: bed or a wooden structure that supports goods in a stable fashion

phenomenon: singular

A short guide on how to write at work

phenomena: plural

pore: to gaze intently
pour: to flow in a continuous stream

ravage: to cause widespread destruction
ravish: to fill with strong emotion or to seize and carry off by force, to rape.
Buildings can be ravaged, but cannot be ravished.

regretfully: when it's your fault or you are full of regret for a decision you made
regrettably: when it's not your fault
Examples:

> *The earthquake regrettably caused widespread damage.*
> *My car accident, regretfully, caused injuries.*

respectively: in the order given
respectfully: with admiration
Examples:

> *The couple's children are named Bob and Sally, 9 and 7 years old, respectively.*
> *The couple's children named Bob and Sally respectfully admired the painting.*

shall: Often poised as a question.
should: Often first person and what a person should do.

tortuous: many twists and turns, not judgmental
torturous: extreme pain as in torture, judgmental
Examples:
The roads on Maui are tortuous.
The kidnappers were torturous.

will: More straightforward and to the point.
would: Would is almost a caveat that something might not happen.
There are some subtle distinctions. Don't fret too much. Use what sounds natural.

Quiz:

Reminder: write answers in shorthand.
1.) What is the difference between good and well?
2.) What is the importance of knowing the difference between good and well?
3.) What is the difference between advice and advise.
4.) Difference between affect and effect?
5.) Difference between aid and aide?
6.) Differences among allusion, delusion and illusion?
7.) Difference between ambiguous and ambivalent?
8.) Differences among assure, ensure and insure?
9.) Differences among average, mean and median?
10.) Difference between bear and bare?
11.) Difference between bring and take?
12.) Differences among censor, censer and censure?
13.) Difference between choose and chose?
14.) Difference between compliment and complement?
15.) Difference between condon and condemn?
16.) Difference between discreet and discrete?
17.) Difference between disinterested and uninterested?
18.) What is important about knowing the difference between disinterested and uninterested?
19.) Correct these sentences:
20.) Difference between incredulous and incredible?
21.) What is irregardless a sign of?
22.) Difference between its and it's?
23.) Difference between lay and lie?

24.) Difference between libel and slander?
25.) Difference between personnel and personal?
26.) Difference between principal and principle?
27.) Difference between stationery and stationary?
28.) Difference between than and then?
29.) What is wrong with this sentence?
He literally jumped over the moon.

For classes, private lessons: Howtowriteatwork@gmail.com

7.

Get me Rewrite!

10-minute read

Editing is painful – especially for the writer.
Believe me, I know. It still hurts when someone decides my work is too long, too obtuse, ungrammatical or worst of all, not worth the time to read it.

Editors can be gruff; it comes with the territory. The more you learn to edit yourself, the less grumpy your editor will be.

PRO TIP 15: Just as you'd look for a hairstylist who will make you look better, seek an editor who will improve your work.

Everyone gets edited. No one writes the perfect first draft.

After Thomas Jefferson wrote the Declaration of Independence, other members of Congress made 86 changes and the original version was cut by a fourth.

When I started as a wee tenderfoot back in the stone age, we used actual typewriters. It was a pain in the ass to correct mistakes. So many sheets of paper were cut and pasted somewhere else that our articles looked like a third-grade project.

Thank God and Bill Gates for the personal computer and Microsoft Word. It is so much easier nowadays to edit our own work.

A short guide on how to write at work

On the flip side, it's also much easier to write too much. What can be said in 500 words may now stretch to 800 words.

In college, English professors would assign maybe a 1,000-word essay on the true meaning of Melville's Moby Dick and students thought, what a pain. So they would fluff up the paper with meaningless gobbly-gook.

In this lesson, we want to learn how to do the opposite. We will use our scalpel like a fine surgeon and remove the dead stuff, the zombie words.

If you write a 500-word message for your co-workers, try cutting it to 300 words. When you look at the penultimate draft of whatever you're writing, see if you can cut 25%. Look for small, unimportant words that you can delete.

Here are 29 tips on how to edit your own work.

1.) Look for adjectives and adverbs. Ask yourself, do you need them?

2.) Look for any use of *you* and try to reword. You is often preachy, particularly when combined with must.

3.) Delete *very*. What do you think when you read the word very? Not much. Very over-used. Writers use very to emphasize the succeeding word. When you see very, cut it out and concentrate on the word it modifies. Make that word the subject of a sentence. Add a description to the word. For example:

Mark is a very exciting player.

An exciting player is Mark.

    4.) Change continuous verbs to active verbs. Take the above example and see the following:

Mark is an exciting player.
Mark excites the crowd by often making three-point shots.
John is working hard.
John works so hard that he skips lunch.

    5.) The *ly* words to avoid:

really
truly
actually
absolutely
extremely

    6.) Search for commas.
Many grammar books will have long, tedious chapters devoted to commas and when to use them. If you have trouble sleeping, check out the debate on the English comma, also known as the serial comma, which shouldn't be confused with a serial killer.
    When commas are spotted, think of them as signals that clauses or phrases are lurking.

    7.) Clauses and phrases are not the main points of the sentence; writers add them to make the sentences full of details. They always deserve our scrutiny to see if they are necessary and modify the correct words.

PRO TIP 16: Make sure the clause or phrase modifies the preceding noun or verb.

8.) Look for the dangling modifiers. For example:

As a project manager, my duties included updating the calendar.

Note the problem? My duties isn't the project manager. You are. Rewrite to say:

As a project manager, I was responsible for updating the calendar.

A tip on how to spot dangler: the sentence starts with an *independent clause, a verb or the phrases it is or there is.*

9.) Prepositions that begin sentences – *as, like, unlike, at, by, in, with* – indicate phrases that can cause problems. When writing the preposition *with*, think of changing to *and, when* or *because.*

10.) Search for *been, by*. They are clues that a passive verb is being used. Rewrite that sentence.

PRO TIP 17: Eliminate as many *beens* as you can. However, sometimes rewriting a sentence to eliminate *been* is awkward. In that case, leave the been.

11.) Keep your paragraphs to one to three sentences. Anything longer is harder to read, particularly on a cell phone.

12.) When an apostrophe *s* is in a sentence, look for any other word that might also need an apostrophe *s*. Take for example this sentence:

Washington's apples are like Michigan.

The apples are compared to Michigan. They should be compared to Michigan's apples. The apostrophe *s* was forgotten. This is the correct way.

Washington's apples are like Michigan's.

13.) Search for *but*. We want to avoid the *yes, but* construction. See if a rewrite is possible to avoid two contradictory thoughts in one sentence. Once you get used to spotting this construction, it's amusing to see it in news articles.

PRO TIP 18: If but is necessary, place a comma before it if the latter clause has a subject and verb.

14.) "Zombie English" means words that are included, but don't tell us much. William Zinsson in his book, "On Writing Well," describes a nice technique: Put brackets around any words or phrases that are not useful. Read the sentence aloud without the bracketed words. If the sentence makes sense, delete the bracketed words.

15.) These words are often used in government and academia. They will also bore the shit out of your readers:

prioritized
procedures
departmental

A short guide on how to write at work

implement
special
enhance
luminous
enthralling

>16.) These are keywords that may signal a re-write.

which
that
there
of
by

>17.) Don't lose the pronoun.

>The pronoun should refer to the noun or person immediately preceding the pronoun. Even professionals forget this rule. Can you spot the two errors in these sentences in a 2017 article in the Wall Street Journal?

Sirius has over 31 million subscribers but doesn't break out Mr. Stern's audience. However he is their biggest star.

>The first mistake: What does *their* refer to? Subscribers or Sirius? The first subject preceeding *their* is Stern. The next possible reference could be *subscribers*. A logical implication is Sirius. However, it's not clear and it causes the reader to hesitate. Don't stop the reader! That's like slamming on the brakes when going 75 mph on the freeway.

>The second mistake: Actually, *their* should be a singular pronoun – *its* -- since it's referring to Sirius, a singular unit.

For classes, private lessons: Howtowriteatwork@gmail.com

18.) In this example, the pronoun shifts:

For a person to bowl well, you must have good form.

Try it this way:

To bowl well, a person must have good form.

PRO TIP 19: Lost pronouns are easy errors to make. When you are editing, use the search box to look for pronouns like *their* or *its* and make sure they refer to the correct item.

19.) I tell my reporters that every word counts. Everyone is super busy and doesn't have time to read words that don't matter.
Note how a fine scalpel can delete these excessive words:

a group of 20 people -- 20 people
a large number of – many
a number of – many
benefit – help
despite the fact that – although
at the present moment – now
following – after
establish the fact that – found
prior to – before
until such time as – until
is indicative – indicates
have an influence – influences
gives consideration – considers
in order to – to
make use of – use
most unique – unique
more complete – complete

A short guide on how to write at work

more perfect – perfect
rather pregnant – pregnant
radio blared loudly – radio blared
clenched teeth tightly – clenched teeth
effortlessly easy – effortlessly
partly flabbergasted – flabbergasted
kind of bold – bold
major breakthrough – breakthrough
big in size – big
few in number – few
eliminate altogether – eliminate
joint cooperation – cooperation
warn in advanced – warn
in spite of the fact that – although
in the vicinity of – near
was witness to – saw
blue in color – blue
strongly demand – demand

20.) What is wrong with this sentence published by the Associated Press?

"We've been amused by amusement parks since the first one opened in Cincinnati in the mid-1800s."

The sentence gives the impression that the writer has been alive for more than 165 years!

I can imagine a tough and gruff editor asking the writer: "Who do you think you are? God?"

A singular author using the plural *we* instead of *I* implies that the writer speaks for more than one person. The use of *we* is a writing trick to make it seem like a lot of people agree with what one person is writing. Such lofty and snobbish writing is usually the domain of kings and queens. Suggested rewrite:

Amusement parks have amused the public since the first one opened in Cincinnati in the mid-1800s.

Note the preceding sentence still has something odd about it – a word echo where the same or similar word is used in the same sentence or nearby. Note the change in amused from the prior sentence.

Amusement parks have entertained the public since the first one opened in Cincinnati in the mid-1800s.

21.) What is wrong with this sentence from an AP story?

About 200 people streamed into Elvis Presley's Memphis after the late singer's wife cut a ribbon and allowed fans to see the $45 million complex for the first time.

The sentence is trying to pack too much information. Let's break down the sentence:

About 200 people
streamed
into Elvis Presley's Memphis
after the late singer's wife
cut a ribbon
and allowed fans
to see the $45 million complex
for the first time.

The sentence has eight ideas. Which phrase makes the reader pause? For me, it's "the late singer's wife."
Is Elvis' wife dead as well?

Whereas we generally want to cut out of the, we don't do so at the expense of clarity. A simple shift ensures Priscilla is still alive (as of this writing anyway). We can easily cut this sentence into two:

About 200 people streamed into Elvis Presley's Memphis, a $45 million complex. Priscilla Presley, the wife of the late singer, cut a ribbon that allowed fans to see for the first time the facilities that resemble an outdoor mall.

22.) Parenthesis takes away from the flow of the writing. They imply a subtle note that you are telling the interested reader a detail or a joke. Try to avoid them.

PRO TIP 19: Write down a list of the errors you are prone to.

23.) When reading a sentence that looks like it was added because it feels obligatory, delete it. I'll never forget my editor asking me when he read a sentence in my article:

"Do you really think this? Do you really believe it?"
"No," I'd answer, "But I feel obligated to put it in."

My editor would cut it out. The message was clear. You as a writer must defend every sentence. If you don't believe it, take it out or show it another way.

PRO TIP 20: Ask yourself constantly, is this word or sentence needed? If not, delete it. Keep rewriting. All writers do this. No one is perfect on the first draft.

24.) Annoying phrases that are too often written or said in the media. Using them is a sure sign that you are trying too hard to look like the media. Ignore these claptraps:

Business enjoying a slump -- no one enjoys a slump.
Taking a profit – TV reporters often use this term to describe a falling stock. However, the reporter doesn't know if the investor made a profit on the stock.
Officials are scrambling – We journalists often laugh about this one. If we couldn't figure out what officials were exactly doing, we said they were scrambling. Whenever I hear or read it, I think of a Monty Python song and dance.
Fret – Headline writers love this work because it's short for worry. However, in my long life, I've never heard someone say he or she is fretting.

25.) Determine if you need the five Ws that are famous in all journalism schools:

who
what
when
where
why

Not everything you write needs each of these Ws. But it's good to ask yourself if the reader would find them handy. I am often amazed at how often highly paid public relations writers of these press releases forget to add these basics.

26.) Don't write "is interesting" Show why it's interesting. For example:

A short guide on how to write at work

The tall man is interesting because he speaks five languages.
The man, who is 7 feet tall, speaks five languages.

27.) Look for the phrase that has of the following a noun ending in *-ion*. The noun can be changed to a gerund, which ends with *-ing*.

creation of the plan
creating the plan
examination of the building
examining the building

Editors often use this technique to shorten sentences.

28.) If you have trouble with a sentence, ask yourself, what is the point of this sentence?
Strip it down to your subject, verb and object to say just that one idea. Then add in adjectives or phrases or clauses as necessary.

29.) What is wrong with this sentence?

Many people believe in extra-terrestrials.

It's a technique used by writers to buttress their points. Whenever I see the word *many*, I ask myself how *many*? Are we talking about four people or 400 or 4,000 or 4 million? Be specific in how many believe. Cite a survey, such as:

Twenty percent of Americans believe in extra-terrestrials, according to a survey.

If a writer cannot quantify the amount in many, don't use it.

Quiz:

Reminder: write answers in shorthand.

1.) How many changes were made to Thomas Jefferson's original version of the Declaration of Independence?

2.) Change the continuous verbs to active verbs in the following sentences:
Julie is an exciting player.
Tom is working hard.

3.) Name five words that end in *ly* to avoid:

4.) What signals do commas send?

5.) What is wrong with the following sentence?

As a project manager, my duties included updating the calendar.

6.) What's a tip on how to spot dangler?

7.) What is implied when using *when* or *by*?

8.) Correct this sentence:

Washington's apples are like Michigan.

9.) What is wrong with these words?

prioritized
procedures
departmental
implement

A short guide on how to write at work

special
enhance
luminous
enthralling

10.) How do you lose a pronoun?

11.) Every word counts. Note how a fine scalpel can delete these excessive words:

a group of 20 people
a large number of
despite the fact that
at the present moment
establish the fact that
until such time as

12. What is wrong with this sentence?

"We've been amused by amusement parks since the first one opened in Cincinnati in the mid-1800s."

13. Why avoid parenthesis?

14. Write down three errors that you consistently make when writing.

15. What are the five famous Ws in journalism?

16. Rewrite to eliminate a word.

creation of the plan

17.) What is wrong with the use of many?

8.

Can I write that?

10-minute read

Many corporations are terrified of publishing anything. Their PR people call me up to complain about my verbs, let alone the stories.

If an executive in its organization opines on a controversial matter, half of the population may not like that opinion. They may form a boycott. A lawyer is often lurking on the sideline, waiting to rush in with a boilerplate lawsuit.

This fear of boycotts or lawsuits explains why so many corporate websites are as dull as a dishrag.

Yet, sometimes corporations must fight back. Famed activist investor Bill Ackman accused nutrition maker Herbalife, where I worked for a few months as a contract writer, of being a fraudulent company. Ackman's accusation was a bit bizarre because Herbalife at that time sold $5 billion worth of products annually and was audited by a Big 4 accounting firm.

So how did Herbalife defend itself? It started a website, therealbillackman.com, that promoted this headline:

BILL ACKMAN HAS MADE SOME JAW-DROPPING MISTAKES.

A short guide on how to write at work

Read and watch what people are saying about Ackman's blunders.

The website contained links to articles from mainstream media like The New York Times and Forbes that questioned Ackman's efforts to destroy Herbalife. When Bill Ackman's name was typed into the Google search, the Herbalife-sponsored website often appeared on the front page as the result of search engine optimization.

To understand why Herbalife could say these things about Ackman, it's important to understand the rules of libel, slander and defamation.

The First Amendment gives every individual the right to express himself or herself. It permits you to say anything about anybody. You don't need permission from the government. There is no overt censorship by the government. In countries like Thailand or Turkey, people are imprisoned because they insulted the wrong person.

In America, you can print anything or say anything.

The issue then is whether the subject doesn't like what you wrote.

Everyone in America also has the right to sue.

The question to ask yourself if you write something negative about a person, is it worth a lawsuit?

If you mention a person in your writing, you should know the American rules of libel. Or for that matter, the rules of libel in the country where you work or where your writing will appear.
Generally, if you write nice things, you will not have a problem.

Here are two points to consider:

a.) Is the person being criticized well known?

People actively involved in public life like movie stars or politicians are less protected in court than say a neighbor down the street.
You can say almost anything you want about famous people in America without fear of a lawsuit. They have fewer rights to complain.

Guess which sentence is likely to result in a lawsuit:

President Trump is a deadbeat who doesn't pay all bills owed to his contractors.
My neighbor John Smith is a deadbeat who doesn't pay all bills owed to his contractors.

You have the right to publish either sentence. Both Trump and Smith have the right to sue you for libel. Trump will have a far less compelling case because he is well known and has been involved in some lawsuits over payments. Smith will likely bring you into court and you will have to prove your sentence. A typical method is not to identify deadbeats. For example:

One of my neighbors is a deadbeat who doesn't pay all bills owed to his contractors.

If you have many neighbors, not one of them can feel like they're identified. Keep in mind that if you only two neighbors, then one of them is likely to feel identified and may sue.
Make the complaint without identifying the person. If in doubt, leave it out.

b.) Is it true?

If you can prove that what you wrote is true, then you can write it. For example, take this sentence:

> *Widget Company Chief Executive Bill Jones is a criminal.*

If that executive was indeed convicted, you will win your lawsuit.

Anything you write can be subject to a lawsuit. However, the ultimate defense is the truth. If you have the facts on your side, you can run with it.

The question then becomes one of cost. Are you willing to spend the money to defend yourself?

Herbalife believed its very existence was threatened by Ackman so the company spent the money to defend itself. It had every right to defend the public accusations made by Ackman. And furthermore, if Ackman had sued, he would have opened his entire practice to a probe by Herbalife attorneys.

Libel is the key reason many companies just don't want to opine on anything. It is why companies will not say anything negative about anybody. They know a lawyer is ready to file a lawsuit.

People and organizations with money thus have an advantage over those without means to pay lawyers.

A key point to remember, if you have money, even just equity in your house, ask yourself before you self-publish on Facebook or Twitter or Instagram or a blog – is it worthwhile for me to risk my assets to opine?

A few other tips:

- You cannot libel a dead person. In other words, the estate of Michael Jackson or Elvis Presley cannot sue you because you wrote something negative about them. This lack of libel is why you'll see the worst stories about dead people.
- You can write about anything submitted to a court as a document because it is in the public domain. I've seen lawyers file nasty lawsuits full of spurious accusations. They aren't hoping to win, but want to be able to air those grievances publicly without fear of libel or slander lawsuits.
- Remember those famous divorce cases where ugly accusations are thrown at each other, especially child abuse? These are attempts by the lawyers to defame the other party and force them to the negotiating table. To some lawyers, the truth doesn't matter.
- It might not be libelous, but it might be in poor taste. If you have second thoughts about something, try inserting the name of someone you like into that sentence and asking yourself if that friend would be offended. If so, take it out. This is where your reputation comes into play.
- If you believe something is libelous from another publication, don't link to it or mention it in your articles. Just because another publication published it doesn't mean you are immune from a lawsuit. Lawyers will seek deeper pockets.
- The person who feels libeled must contact you to demand a correction or retraction within a certain time frame. A correction

often lessens the case of the person who feels libeled.

- Libel is damaging one person's reputation in print and sometimes on recorded TV shows. Slander is verbally damaging a person's reputation, say on live television. Look smart. Never say.

He slandered me in the newspaper.

The following is a real example of an investor named Howard Marks who was mad about the person he invested with, Hilary Novelle Hahn. Marks wrote a blog that in my opinion libeled Hahn. However, here's why Howard would win a libel lawsuit:

> Venture capitalist Howard Marks made a startling discovery when one of the people he invested in, Hilary Novelle Hahn, founder of a company called the **Style Club**, appeared on the popular TV show Shark Tank.
> During the TV show, Marks learned that Hahn had switched the company name and Marks was no longer an investor. How mad was Marks? He took her reputation and tossed it around like a shark eating a piece of freshly cut meat:
> "I invested in her company because I liked her thesis and thought she was smart and honest. This clearly has not been proven true," Marks wrote on his Linkedin blog. He also accused Hahn of "having stolen the assets" of the company he invested in.
> Clearly, this blog damaged the reputation of Hahn. Marks says he's made more than 60 venture capital investments, which gives him a high level of credibility. Anyone who reads this blog would question whether to invest with Hahn or permit her to run a company. Marks is now

exposed to a potential libel lawsuit. Corporations and sometimes the press avoid such articles not because they are wrong, but because they don't want the added expense of a lawsuit.

The question for Hahn, a former teen pop singer who performed the opening act for the likes of Christina Aguilera and Destiny's Child, is whether she should sue. A mediocre lawyer will happily take her money and tell her she has a good case. A good libel lawyer will advise her of the obstacles.

Marks has two things going for him. The best defense is the truth. His blog makes a compelling case and Hahn would have a lot of explaining to do in any courtroom.

The second is deep pockets. Marks' LinkedIn page said he was one of the founders of Activision, one of the world's largest video-game makers. In other words, Marks probably did well enough to blog what he wanted without worrying about the cost of a lawsuit.

A plaintiff lawyer could make Marks cringe a bit with some of the assertions in the article. But will Hahn want to spend the money and time on a libel lawsuit?

Hahn will have a tough time winning the lawsuit for these two reasons. Hahn swam with the sharks and she got bit.

I know some people who think that everything should be texted or emailed or placed on Facebook for discussion. However, there are sensitive areas that writing cannot compete. When you are writing for one or two people, often you cannot see the reader's facial expression or hear the nuances in their voices.

In matters of sensitivity, don't write. Instead, call or visit the person. You'll be able to pick up more information than with a written sentence.

A short guide on how to write at work

Earl Long, a governor of Louisiana in the 1930s and brother of the famous Huey Long, had a wise saying on sensitive issues:

Don't write anything you can phone. Don't phone anything you can talk. Don't talk anything you can whisper. Don't whisper anything you can smile. Don't smile anything you can nod. Don't nod anything you can wink.

Quiz:
Reminder: write answers in shorthand.
1.) Why are many corporate websites so boring?
2.) Can you libel a dead person? What does that mean?
3.) What is the difference between libel and slander?

9.

Headlines – Read all about them!

5-minute read

Here's a secret about Wall Street. Stories don't cause the stocks to fall or rise. Headlines do. That's because traders on Wall Street often know intimately the story already. It's a headline like Apple beats analysts' consensus that moves the stock up. I myself have written headlines that have moved a stock by hundreds of million of dollars, and sometimes billions.

Headlines are crucial to telling your story.

If you wrote a beautiful article, what if no one read it?

Bummers!

Why?

It starts with the headline.

Maybe the headline wasn't interesting or gave the wrong impression.

Everyone reads a headline to determine if they want to read more. Even newspaper publishers seldom read every single article in their publications. They don't have the time, but they look at the headlines.

A headline is more difficult than it appears. First, it should be short. If you wrote a 400-word memo, use at most 10 words for the headline.

Yes, many things deserve to be mentioned in a headline. However, like a two-seater car, not everyone gets a ride. Focus on the most important point.

Let's break down what works and doesn't work in a headline.

PRO TIP 21: Think of the subject line of an email or a tweet as a headline. It's amazing how many people don't.

What works?

In the old days, sales at newsstands told media executives how popular certain issues were. If certain celebrities were on the cover, sales popped. The same occurred if certain words were used like war or sex or scandal or disaster. A celebrity acting poorly? The old cliché is true – everyone stops to see a train wreck.

In the 2000s when newsstand sales fell off a cliff and the Internet took off in popularity, it became possible to measure the success of a headline by how many clicks it generated.
In the beginning, clicks were a rough, imperfect gauge also used by Internet firms to justify advertising costs. I remember a Bloomberg article that told of click farms in India where children did nothing more than click on advertisements to justify higher fees for the Internet company.

Still, an editor and reporter know a story that had 500 clicks wasn't as popular as one with 10,000 clicks. We learned that certain words drew traffic among our Wall Street readers such as bonuses (as in JPMorgan bonuses to rise 15% this year) and beats (as in Widget Company beats forecasts). Sometimes, esoteric subjects like day care in Manhattan generated high clicks.

The word sex almost always sells, as in:

Celebrity Y Caught on Sex Tapes

One truism is that including Warren Buffett in the headline is a sure winner among business readers. Everyone wants to read what the world's most famous investor is doing. Some Bloomberg editors became notorious for trying every possible way to get Buffett into the headline, even if he was barely mentioned in the story.

That leads to my next point: the headline must deliver what is promised or readers will ignore your headlines in the future. If the story is about sex or Warren Buffett, that story better include sex or Warren Buffett. Famous names and companies make news. Which of these stories would you read?

Peter J. Brennan Names his Favorite Stocks
Warren Buffett Names his Favorite Stocks
Widget Company Declares Giant Dividend
Apple Declares Giant Dividend

Start the headline with the famous name. Don't bury the name such as this one:

Favorite Stocks Named by Warren Buffett.

The problem is two-fold: Not only is Buffett buried, it's a passive headline. Now instead of Buffett, try inserting your CEO's name. Everyone in your company, if they know what is good for career building, will read a message from your CEO.

A second technique is to put a superlative in the headline like first:

Chicago Cubs Win First World Championship in 108 Years

A short guide on how to write at work

The first 6 words are the view in prime real estate. Don't put the equivalent of a bookshelf to block that view. Read how the following headline buries the most important part:

Based in Wrigley Field, Chicago Cubs Win a Game After Rain Delay

A technique I like to use is to pretend I'm meeting the president of the United States in the elevator, and I have 10 seconds to say something interesting.
What would I say? My goal is to get that person's attention and make them want to continue the conversation with me. So instead of saying:

I just heard an interesting person name his favorite stocks.

Try this:

Warren Buffett just told me his five favorite stocks

Another technique is to write headlines in the present or future tense. This technique gives the impression that the news is fresh and not old. Magazines like to keep their articles in the present tense to give the impression that the news isn't old. Slimy? More like a little white lie.
Be sure to leave out articles like *a* and ***the***. This technique saves space.
The following section has actual headlines pulled off press releases written in 2017. I rewrote them to give readers of the possibilities and insights on how to look at these headlines. Consider doing the same for your Tweets or the subject lines of your emails. The symbol TK is a journalism acronym for

information "to come." In these cases, I would look in the press release for such information or consult the person who would know the answers to my questions.

1.)
Animal Protein Market 2017 Global Industry Size, Share, Growth, Outlook and Forecast to 2021: MarketReportsOnline

Insights: Tease the reader with more information on why this is a growing market.

Animal Protein Market Forecast to Grow TK% to $TK by 2021

2.)
Denial Events, in Association with Skydeck Experiences, Presents an Exclusive Curated Adventure Under the Electric Skies of EDCLV17

Insights: Denial Events is a terrible name for a headline. Even though Denial is the name of the company, readers will first think they must give up something pleasurable whereas this press release is trying to give pleasure to those who watch. What is the meaning of the acronym EDCLV17? It may be well known among the people hosting the event, but newcomers may not realize what the acronym stands for and thus ignore this event. Don't use an acronym unless is well known like the FBI.

The Exciting 'Adventure Under the Electric Skies' Scheduled for TK

3.)

A short guide on how to write at work

IPC Collaborates with OneAsia to Provide Financial Market Connectivity into China

Insights: Collaborates has two problems: it's too long of a word for a headline and it implies a traitor. Connectivity is a jargon word that can signify many different things.

IPC, OneAsia Join Forces to Provide Financial Information on China

4.)
Astellas Announces Record Number of Abstracts highlighting Breadth and Depth of Oncology Portfolio Data to be Presented at 2017 ASCO Annual Meeting

Insights: Note how the original headline has 22 words. I cut it in half to 11. Headlines need to be precise. If the headline writer of this press release isn't precise, an editor at a publication will do the cutting.

Astellas Reports Most Abstracts Ever on Oncology Data at Annual Meeting

5.)
New Book Outlines Comprehensive Solutions on the Environment

Insights: Words have meaning. An outline is a rough sketch. Comprehensive is complete, including many elements of something. Together, these words form an oxymoron. Furthermore, comprehensive contains too many letters and is jargon.

For classes, private lessons: Howtowriteatwork@gmail.com

New Book Profiles Solutions to Environmental
Problems

6.)
"Investing in infrastructure is a guarantee of job
creation," said the governor of Sao Paulo in the LIDE
Brazilian Investment Forum in NYC

Insights: It looks like someone just copied a quote in
the press release and inserted it into the headline.
Starting a headline with a gerund or a quote isn't a
good idea. In this case, the title of the speaker is the
most important.

Sao Paulo Governor Says Infrastructure Investment
Guarantees Job Creation

7.)
Empower Energies Adds Industry Leaders in Sales
and Operations as Company Ramps Up
Development, Acquisition and Construction of
Commercial & Industrial Solar Projects

Insights: What is Empower announcing? It seems
like new executives, although "industry leaders"
could imply it's acquiring companies. This is where
the headline writer must get information from the
press release. There's a word echo: industry and
industrial. Too many words, 23, are in the headline. I
cut to nine words.

Empower Energies Hires Executives to Ramp
Commercial Solar Projects

8.)

Big Data in the Automotive Industry: 2017-2030 - $2.8 billion Opportunities, challenges, Strategies & Forecasts – Research and Markets

Insights: In a headline, every letter counts. Cut automotive to auto. Lead with auto industry because it is a huge industry in the U.S. with many potential readers. What does $2.8 billion represent? Big Data's annual sales in 2017 or in 2030? Go with the forecast for 2030 because the number should be bigger and more impressive. Here is a waste of eight words in the headline: "Opportunities, challenges, Strategies & Forecasts – Research and Markets"

Auto Industry's Use of `Big Data' Forecast to Grow to $tk Billion by 2030

9.)
Building Blocks for the Feed Industry: Oxea Expands Production Capabilities for Butyric Acid and Propionic Acid

Insights: Why is building blocks in the headline? Capabilities is unneeded. Can we reduce acid to one mention? Cut out *and*.

Oxea Expands Production of Butyric, Propionic Acids for Feed Industry

10.)
Global Online Survey Software Market – Analysis, Technologies & Forecasts to 2021 – Iincreased Use of Online Survey Software Among SMBs—Research and Markets

Insights: The original headline is an example of a waste of the first 11 words. The headline writer is blocking the view of what is occurring. Increased is past tense, which shouldn't be used in headlines and certainly not for a forecast. Furthermore, SMBs may mean something different so don't use this acronym. I assume it's small to medium size businesses. Since we don't have room for small to medium size, I shortened it to smaller, which could be either small or medium-size. Then we go into the press release or report to show how much this industry is growing on an annual basis. Is the growth in sales or the number of surveys? The press release should tell us. Furthermore, everyone in business is looking for growth industries, which are sales climbing 15% or more annually. The 15% signals sales will double in five years. If the growth is below 15%, I suggest looking for a different statistic to make your readers go wow!

Smaller Businesses to Boost Online Survey Software by tk%

Quiz:
Reminder: write answers in shorthand.
1.) How many words should a headline have at most?
2.) What is important about a headline?
3.) What should be the first word of a headline?
4.) Why are many media headlines in the present or future tense when the action happened in the past?
5.) When should you use an acronym in a headline?
6.) Should you start a headline with a gerund? Why or why not?

10.

The Checklist

Three-minute read

One of the great things about modern technology is the ability to use the search function in a word document. Of course, you should painstakingly read each sentence. Then once you do, use the search in your Word document to look for common errors.

For example, say you wrote a 500-word paper. To find out how many sentences you wrote, put a period into the search button. Say your 500-word paper has 40 periods, then you know more or less that you have 40 sentences, or about 12.5 words per sentence. Say you only have 15 periods, that implies you are writing 33 words a sentence. Yes, averaging 33 words per sentence is long.

Type the word *is* into the search button. If you have 50 or more uses of *is* in your 200-word note, then you know you are not using enough active verbs. Not every sentence needs an active verb. Try to see if you can cut the use of *is* in half to say 25 times.

Using the previous nine chapters as a guide, here is a checklist of things to look out for in your writing. Print it out when have finished your memo, article, email,

blog or whatever you have written. After
you have searched, put a checkmark next to
it.

	Checked?
Chapter 1 – before you start	
What is the point?	
Correct word count	
Chapter 2 – tenses	
tense consistent	
tense shifting	
Chapter 3 – verb subject agreement	
subject identified in each sentence	
main verb identified in each sentence	
object identified in each sentence	
one idea per sentence	
any sentence over 20 words	
more than 1 clause in a sentence	
Chapter 4 – techniques inside sentences	
active verb	
passive verb -- was, were	
by	
been, be	
phrase identified	
clause identified	
as, like, unlike removed from beginning of sentence	

commas correct	
dangling modifier	
of the	
there	
its, their, ours	
apostrophe	
meaning of words	
parallelism spotted	
and	
but	
split infinitive	
word echo	
adjectives, adverbs trimmed	
very, really, deleted	
double negative avoided	
you removed	
Chapter 5 – overall techniques	
characters described	
names doublechecked for spelling	
sentence longer than 16 words rewritten	
audience known	
quotes lively	
acronyms obvious	
opinions checked	
Chapter 6 – words to avoid	
really, truly, actually, absolutely, extremely	
beens, be	
Chapter 7 - rewrite	

find word echo	
delete zombie words	
delete boring words	
excessive words deleted	
words to signal rewrite: which, that, there, by, of	
apostrophes correctly added	
adverbs also, only, not, however in front of verbs	
parallelism: either, neither, or nor	
rollercoaster words: over, under, above, below	
interesting as word found and described instead	
delete: very	
delete: really, truly, actually, absolutely, extremely	
that without commas	
which with commas	
lost pronouns	
delete parenthesis	
five Ws: who, what, were, why, when	
adverb with -ly ending sentence changed	
Chapter 8 – legal	
offensive to someone	
if in doubt, leave it out	
Chapter 9 – headlines	
present tense	
delete a, the	
famous name	
headline reflects main point	

A short guide on how to write at work

11.

Tips used by professional writers

5-minute read

PRO TIP 1: Write about subjects that you know. Don't opine on popular issues in the media that you may not be fully versed in. Professional columnists are paid to write about controversy and even to create it. Even so, they've learned how to nuance a sentence. Most columnists have years at their professions and make it look much easier than it really is. They've learned how to avoid the easy mistakes that can undermine an opinion.

PRO TIP 2: If you want to mix it up, use short sentences with a few long sentences thrown in. Don't use long sentences with a few short ones.

PRO TIP 3: I've seen high-level executives inspired to write an article of 1,000 to 2,000 words and then expect their companies to publish them on the company website. Coordinate with your marketing department before spending the time and effort to write an article.

PRO TIP 4: If you write a book, you will be introduced at public forums as the person who wrote the book on subject X. However, don't consider a book a future big revenue stream. Instead, think of a book on your field of expertise as a good way to market your career. And be pleasantly surprised if people read your book.

PRO TIP 5: Adjectives are great for creative writing. Try to avoid them in business writing. See Chapter 4.

PRO TIP 6: Pronouns sometimes get too far away from the word they replace. Always doublecheck that your pronoun is referring to the correct subject. See Chapter 7.

PRO TIP 7: The exception to Pro Tip 6 is the indefinite pronoun, which doesn't need to refer to a prior subject. See Chapter 3. Indefinite pronouns include: *anyone, each, every, everyone, nobody, no one, nothing, someone, both, few, several, many, all, any, enough, more, most, none, plenty, some.*

PRO TIP 8: Just like adjectives, try to avoid adverbs.

PRO TIP 9: If you must use an adverb, don't use it with a hyphen.

PRO TIP 10: Shifts in tenses cause many writers to get bogged down. Writing in the past tense will save you a lot of grief. See Chapter 2 for a reminder.

PRO TIP 11: Writers strive for active voices. See Chapter 4.

PRO TIP 12: Seek passive verbs and destroy them when possible. A key to finding them is to look for was or is followed by a verb ending with -ed. Example:

> *The actor was ridiculed.*

Change to:

> *Critics ridiculed the actor.*

PRO TIP 13: If your company has a problem you want to downplay, use the passive voice to describe it. For example, in the active voice, you might write:

> *Widget Company manufactured products that injured a few consumers.*

Passive voice:

*A few consumers were injured by products
manufactured by Widget Company.*

See how Widget Company is buried at the end of the
sentence? See Chapter 4 for more tips.

PRO TIP 14: Pay close attention to the verb-subject
agreement. See Chapter 3.

PRO TIP 15: Clauses get many writers into trouble.
Try to avoid them. If you use them, make sure they
are modifying the correct noun or verb. Commas are
often clues to finding clauses. See Chapter 4.

PRO TIP 16: Try to avoid *but.* It often results in
a *yes, but* sentence construction that can confuse the
reader. Which side of the issue are you the writer on?
When you finish what you are writing, look back to
see how many buts are in your story. Try to cut them
out as much as possible. The same goes for *and.* The
word and is a signal that the sentence may be getting
too long. Once you get used to this, it's fun to read
newspaper stories for the *yes, but* construction.

PRO TIP 17: Recognize when to use the
article. *A* or *an* denotes one of many. *The* emphasizes
the noun following it as the important one. Look at
this example:

> *Apple is a computer company.*

or

> *Apple is the computer company.*

The latter sentence gives more importance to Apple.
One of the fun things about being a writer is deciding
what to emphasize.

PRO TIP 18: Dangling modifiers cause problems for many writers. Pay close attention to avoid them. See Chapter 4.

PRO TIP 19: Some phrases look simple but are easy to mix verbs and meaning. See Chapter 5.

PRO TIP 20: Keep sentences short. Under 25 words. Each one.

PRO TIP 21: The hundreds of different irregular verbs have odd tenses that can screw you as easily as a tax bill. Rather than intimidate you with dozens of examples, stay in the past tense.

PRO TIP 22: Be aware of tenses that shift within your sentences or your story.

PRO TIP 23: A word about *there*. If the sentence begins with there, it's a sign of a weak sentence. Look for the subject after the verb. Rewrite to put the subject before the verb. If you must use there, make sure the verb agrees in *there is* or *there are*:

> *There's two ways people achieve no-closing costs mortgages.*
> *There are two ways people achieve no-closing costs mortgages.*

A simple rewrite:

> *People can obtain a no-closing costs mortgages in two ways.*

PRO TIP 24: Do a search of your document. If you find too many words like *nonetheless, however* or *still*, you are pulling your reader in too many directions and giving too many options.

PRO TIP 25: Some elite colleges teach the double negative as a delightful way to be snobbish and the leaving the intended victim unaware of the condescension.

PRO TIP 26: Everyone loves seeing their name in print in a good way. If you have a chance to mention someone in writing, do so. And if possible, mention their spouses or children or other relatives you have met. Always triple-check that you spelled their names correctly, which is a sign that you care about them.

PRO TIP 27: Try to avoid all commas in your first sentence because they indicate a clause that will take away from your main point.

PRO TIP 28: If your first sentence is longer than 16 words, consider rewriting it. Just one subject, one verb and one object.

PRO TIP 29: Well educated people pay attention to this difference between *disinterested*, which is unaffected, and *uninterested,* which is uncaring.

PRO TIP 30: When editors go nuts, consider their plight. It is their job to catch mistakes and if they miss enough mistakes, they are fired, which explains why they are a grumpy lot. Sometimes they are relieved to have caught the error, sort of like catching a grenade that is accidently dropped. Do the editor a favor by asking them to explain the problem to you. Then make a mental note not to repeat that error.

PRO TIP 31: Remember a biweekly salary means you'll get paid 26 times a year while a semiweekly salary means 24 paychecks!

PRO TIP 32: Instead of thinking of your editor as a person who will put you down, look for an editor who will improve your work.

PRO TIP 33: Make sure the clause or phrase modifies the preceding noun or verb.

PRO TIP 34: Eliminate as many *beens* as you can.

PRO TIP 35: If *but* is necessary, place a comma before it if the latter clause has a subject and verb.

PRO TIP 36: Lost pronouns are easy errors to make. Include who in the search box for a final check.

PRO TIP 37: Write down a list of the errors you are prone to.

PRO TIP 38: Ask yourself constantly, is this word or sentence needed? If not, delete it. Keep rewriting. All writers do this. No one is perfect on the first draft.

PRO TIP 39: Think of the subject line of an email or a tweet as a headline. It's amazing how many people don't.

PRO TIP 40: Boredom is a wonderful human trait. It's a signal that you are tired of doing something the same way. We writers worry that artificial intelligence will take over the writing of our articles. It's already happening in some areas like stock coverage. However, machines don't get bored. They can repeat themselves to exhaustion. Use boredom as a hint that it's time to find another subject to write about.

PRO TIP 41: A short comment about a sentence fragment. The previous sentence is a fragment. It looks like a sentence, but it doesn't have a verb. It is the opposite of a run-on sentence.

Wrapping Things Up

You've reached the end. Yeah!

I am available as a ghostwriter, an editor or a copy editor. If you're interested, email me at:

Howtowriteatwork@gmail.com

Now go out there and tackle some nouns and verbs and great sentences.

To quote an AI blurb -- you've got this!